CREATIVE HEALING

An Introduction to Joseph B. Stephenson's "Hands On" Healing

PATRICIA B. BRADLEY, Editor

COVER SYMBOL EXPLAINED

This symbol, used on the cover, was designed by Mr. Stephenson in the early 1930's. It was used in a small brochure to encourage peaceful, like-minded people to join together in a Silent Circle of Truth and Light.

Mr. Stephenson saw this as the beginning of a NEW ERA and felt that a critical number of self-chosen people would "act as leaven to improve the world".

He used the symbol again at the top a letter to his students, commencing on November 1, 1946. This letter of acceptance into his circle of Creative Healing, advised students to use their new knowledge wisely and to cultivate "naturalness" in their lives.

Library of Congress Catalog Card Number 94-075748
ISBN-13: 978-0-916192-51-8

COPYRIGHT NOTICE
Copyright © 1988 and 1994 by the Joseph B. Stephenson Foundation, Inc. All rights reserved World wide. No part of this publication may be copied or distributed, transmitted, stored in a retrieval system, or translated into any human or computer language, in any form or by any means, electronic, mechanical, magnetic, manual, or otherwise, or disclosed to third parties without express written permission of The Joseph B. Stephenson Foundation, Inc.

Published by LP Publications
7119 E. Shea Blvd
Suite 109 PMB 418
Scottsdale, AZ 85254-6107

DEDICATION

This book is dedicated to
MABEL GUNDERSON YOUNG

who studied, performed,
and actively taught Creative Healing
for over 25 years
bringing
wellness and inspiration
to many people.

ACKNOWLEDGEMENTS

Grateful appreciation is extended to:

Mabel Gunderson Young — *for encouragement & corrections.*
Norma Flynn — *for her artistry.*

Louise Hunt
Stanley Bertsch
Sharon Bertsch
for proofreading, accuracy & suggestions.

John Bradley — *for word processing & patience.*

CONTENTS

TITLE PAGE	i
COVER SYMBOL EXPLAINED COPYRIGHT AND PUBLISHER'S NOTICE	ii
DEDICATION	iii
ACKNOWLEDGEMENTS	iv
CONTENTS	v
PRECAUTION and DISCLAIMER	vi
LIST OF TREATMENTS In sequence taught by Stephenson	vii
PREFACE	ix
BASIC INFORMATION	11
CREATIVE HEALING TREATMENTS	15
ABOUT MR. STEPHENSON	100
INDEX	103
FRONT OF THE BODY Creative Healing Locations	105
BACK OF THE BODY Creative Healing Locations	107

PRECAUTION AND DISCLAIMER

A VERY IMPORTANT MESSAGE TO THE READER

The Joseph B. Stephenson Foundation Inc., a not-for-profit California corporation, is not a clinic and does not perform treatments. Anyone using these techniques as treatment or therapy must already have the appropriate license to do so, depending on their location and application.

The Joseph B. Stephenson Foundation does not qualify a person for such licensing. Students must understand that Creative Healing makes no claims for diagnosing or curing diseases. For diagnosing, prescribing or curing of disease, a medical doctor or other licensed practitioner should be consulted.

To contact The Joseph B. Stephenson Foundation:
creativehealing@hotmail.com

To learn more:
www.stephensonscreativehealing.org

LIST OF TREATMENTS

In the sequence taught by Mr. Stephenson and in the sequence presented in this book:

General Treatment	15	Kidneys	65
Sinus, Hayfever and Catarrh	17	Sciatica	68
		Constipation	72
Adenoids	19	Hemorrhoids	73
Hearing and Antrums	20	Bearing Down Pain	75
Tonsils	22	Abdominal Massage	76
Strep Throat	23	Liver	77
Laryngitis	24	Gall Bladder	78
The Voice	25	Pancreas	80
The Eyes	26	Spleen	81
The Face	29	Digestive Tune-up	82
Night Sweats	32	Ulcerated Stomach	83
High Blood Pressure	33	Bed Wetting, Weak Bladder	85
Pain Between the Shoulders	36	Female Disorders	86
Common Headaches	38	Fallen Stomach	91
Epilepsy	39	Reproductive Organs	92
Migraine	40	Prostate	93
Pain in the Arms	41	Crippled Legs	94
Pain in the Elbow	44	Cartilage of the Knee	96
Wrist and Hand Circulation	46	Ankle Filter	97
		Sprained Ankle	98
Heart	48	Bunions	99
Inward Goiter	56		
High and Short Breathing	59		
Pneumonia and Lung Congestion	62		
Asthma	63		

PREFACE

Creative Healing would have been lost when its founder Mr. Stephenson left the planet in 1956 had it not been for two very dedicated people. These two were chosen by Mr. Stephenson and both were committed to carry on his work, which they each did in his and her individual manner.

MABEL GUNDERSON YOUNG, to whom this book is dedicated, chose to teach the primary lessons found in this book as Mr. Stephenson had done—ten lessons of two hours each. The treatments in this book are arranged in the sequence as taught by Mr. Stephenson

Mr. Stephenson felt that "anyone with willing hands and a good heart" could learn these basic lessons. Those persons who, in addition, travel the "Path of Wisdom" far enough would develop a "Positive Mind". This would enable them to develop and apply their own 'creativity' to the basic work.

Mabel studied all of Mr. Stephenson's teachings reducing them to the FOUR PRINCIPLES underlying all the work. She then wrote a brief explanation of each treatment. Since Mr. Stephenson had written nothing about Creative Healing methods, he was very pleased and suggested these writings be published.

A small booklet, copyrighted in 1951, was printed and used by early students. A pamphlet showing the 52 points on the human form where Creative Healing treatments are applied was crafted by Mr. Stephenson himself. These were the first publications about Creative Healing.

PREFACE

Certain terms reflect the understanding and terminology of an earlier time, i.e. "catarrh" and "hay fever germ". and may be found throughout the text. Nevertheless, the treatments described have been effective.

Mabel wrote to her students at one point, "As you know this wonderful and efficient method of healing is copyrighted under the title "CREATIVE HEALING". It seems that the time is not yet here when we can openly and proudly use that term. We can take comfort in being known by what we do rather than by what we might call ourselves."

Mr. Stephenson advised his students to do their work quietly and prophesied in the 1940s that Creative Healing would not be publicly accepted for another fifty years. I believe the time is here.

Patricia B. Bradley, Editor

BASIC INFORMATION
including the 4 principles of CH

We are living in an exciting age where many orthodoxies are being questioned, where we are seeking for answers to inequities and where there is greater understanding and appreciation of that which is natural. This work is offered in the hope that it will contribute something of great benefit to the common good—the well-being and health of the planet and its peoples.

There is nothing new under the sun and Creative Healing is not a new concept. It was used in ages past but lost, according to its founder, Joseph B. Stephenson. Since the world is now entering a New Age in which minds will be more attuned to everything natural, this work will become known and used to bridge the gap between science and wholeness.

The Joseph B. Stephenson Foundation has already accumulated a large body of work and this book is only an introduction. An Introductory Course would teach enough for the average person to take care of most of his or her family's needs.

Mr. Stephenson, the founder of Creative Healing in this century, was so far advanced as a healer that when necessary the patient's body became transparent to him. Consequently his diagnosis was perfect and his healing consistent. The method he perfected is so efficient that even a beginner experiences wonderful results. The very simplicity of the method makes it difficult for many people to accept.

His legacy to our generation reminds us that the

body is created and equipped to do its own healing. Completing an introductory Creative Healing course will give one a different way of "seeing" the body and a different concept of the Art of Healing. Creative Healing gives us the knowledge of vital nerve centers hidden away in little cavities or dents in the bones where repositioning, stimulation, drainage or other corrections will hasten the healing process.

Another example of how Creative Healing works with nature is the use of gravity. In many treatments the patient sits in an upright position. Gravity works for us in establishing drainage in the throat, draining excess blood from the head and in treating kidneys, for example.

The term, "Life Force" is a cover-all word for **identifiable** operations like blood flow, nerve systems, etc. and **UNidentified** operations like the flow of energy, the return of strength, the uses of all internal space, etc.

Our body's very efficient "manufacturing plant" handles the food we eat in an automatic and beneficial way. Of course a good diet is important. Mr. Stephenson noted that if the body is functioning properly, it can accustom itself to many different types of food—as witness the dietary habits of people from various parts of the world. Our work in Creative Healing is to see that the body functions as perfectly as possible.

BASIC INFORMATION

In an introductory Creative Healing course we learn techniques—how to use our hands—how to place our hands when massaging—to feel and release contractions and how to use the hands to create a vacuum. The sequence of this book essentially follows Mr. Stephenson's unique method of teaching the work—from head to foot.

The use of olive oil was recommended by Mr. Stephenson for all treatments. It acts as protective gloves, making the treatments pleasant and easy to receive.

The work becomes more truly creative when we have mastered these techniques. Then our hands will work for us so efficiently that our minds will not constantly have to remind them what to do.

It is wonderful to know that while we are helping others with this work, we are helping ourselves to grow—to allow our minds to expand and become more truly creative while our hands become ever more skillful.

FOUR BASIC PRINCIPLES

As you review the work covered in this book you will notice that **FOUR BASIC PRINCIPLES** are observed when giving treatments:

1. To **MAINTAIN NORMAL TEMPERATURE** of the body it may be necessary to remove heat. In other conditions it may be necessary to add heat.

2. The principle of **CREATING A VACUUM** is frequently used to establish drainage from glands or organs that have become congested.

3. The **REPOSITIONING SUBSTANCE** principle or putting dislocations back into place is used in many instances, ie. with soft tissue that has slipped or in lifting organs which may have prolapsed. To realize that nature works with us and knows what needs to be done, makes our work comparatively simple.

4. To **REMOVE CONGESTION** is the fourth principle. It is done by the 'breaking up' movement performed by a circular motion of the fingers. The surface tissue contacted moves with the fingers as they move. This creates a penetrating action and, though it is performed very gently, the effect can break up and disperse internal congestion.

CREATIVE HEALING TREATMENTS
THE GENERAL TREATMENT

The General Treatment is given to everyone—sometimes as a specific treatment in itself or as a preliminary or a follow up to other treatments.

Creative Healing makes good use of the fact that man is endowed with an upright spine and for this treatment the patient will be sitting in an upright position. You will become more and more aware of the effectiveness of this posture.

Sit quietly behind the patient and place your hands on the patient's shoulders. In doing so you will become aware of nervous tensions, vibrations and sometimes heat. The first part of the treatment is like a massage as you work to loosen the muscles which lie parallel to the spine and between the spine and the shoulder blades. Let your fingertips penetrate this muscle and then follow through with the palm of your hand. It will be necessary to support your patient's body with one hand so that you can massage with the other—alternating first on one side of the spine, then the other. This helps train both your hands.

Now you are ready to loosen the area around the crest of the shoulder blades. Emotional, mental and physical tensions accumulate in this network of nerves. By standing up, your shoulders will provide strength as you use your thumbs and/or fingertips as a unit to relax the muscles around the shoulder blades, exerting pressure from the sides toward the center back.

THE GENERAL TREATMENT

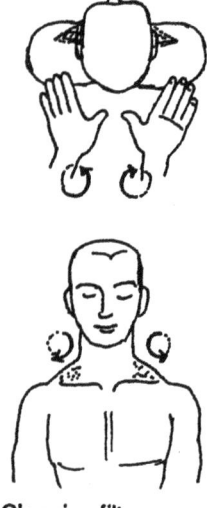

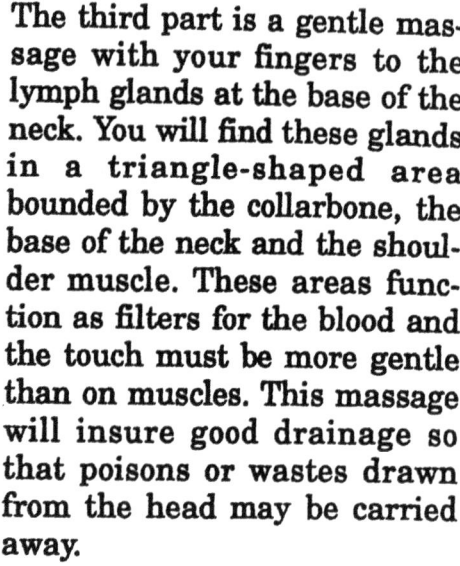

Cleaning filter area

The third part is a gentle massage with your fingers to the lymph glands at the base of the neck. You will find these glands in a triangle-shaped area bounded by the collarbone, the base of the neck and the shoulder muscle. These areas function as filters for the blood and the touch must be more gentle than on muscles. This massage will insure good drainage so that poisons or wastes drawn from the head may be carried away.

Fourth, the forefingers are used to drain downward along the side of the neck to break up obstructions.

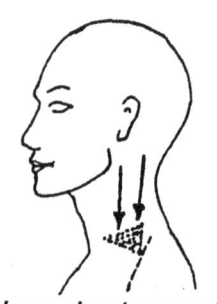

Vacuuming downward

As a guide, this treatment should take from 3 to 5 minutes, but may be longer depending on the built-in tension in the neck and shoulders.

You may not always follow this exact sequence as you consider the needs of each patient. For example, a person with lower back pain must be given relief for that first and put at ease, before doing anything else.

See the HIGH BLOOD PRESSURE treatment for further applications of this treatment.

SINUS, HAY FEVER AND CATARRH

The complete treatment for these ailments takes only a few minutes but as in so many other treatments we must remember that we are only setting the healing process in motion. Nature is equipped to do her own healing—our duty is to start the process.

The germs that come to life in all of these cases are self-contained along with many other organisms in the area of the forehead.

The SINUS germ lives in the cavity underneath the eyebrows. Certain conditions will bring it to life and it begins to bore up into the arch of the brow, giving much pain.

The real sinus germ works in shifts—for instance it may start at 7 a.m. and work for 2 or 3 hours. Then it may fall asleep and not come to life again for 24 hours. The sinus patient may be aware that the extreme pain of sinusitis is not continuous.

The method of treatment is to create a vacuum for drainage, by massaging (upward only) from the bridge of the nose to the hairline, using two fingers on each hand, one hand following the other.

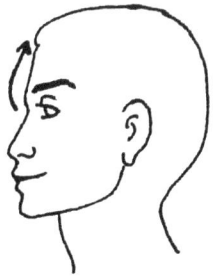

18   SINUS, HAY FEVER AND CATARRH

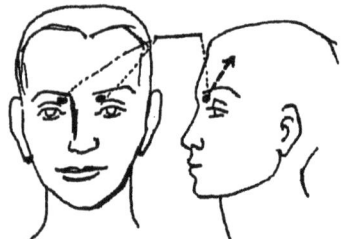

This gentle massage will draw the germs upward to the little cavities found under each eyebrow about 3/4 of an inch from the center of the nose bone. Press these cavities, gently and quickly the first time.

The sequence is repeated three times with increasing pressure to the cavities. The number of treatments will vary with the person.

A word of caution if the sinus condition is one of longstanding. If you see a blue line on the forehead just above the brows, do not press the cavities. There may be so many active germs that the bone structure of the brow has been honeycombed and the pressure of your finger could collapse it. Fortunately these cases are few and far between.

The HAY FEVER germ is a different one but it is in the same region as the sinus and the method of treatment is exactly the same. This germ may be brought to life by many things, such as flowers, weeds, dust, aromas, etc., when the internal conditions of the body and mind are receptive.

CATARRH* on the other hand, is brought on by a draft. Catarrh and post-nasal drip will respond to the same treatment described above. It is comforting to know that these treatments may be self-administered.

---

* Inflammation of mucous membranes of nose and throat with a post-nasal, mucous drip.

ADENOIDS 19

The adenoid glands are part of the body's first line of defense. They constantly expel a poison to combat foreign germs that are breathed in through the nose, the natural inhaling channel.

Adenoid trouble gives the nose a flattened, puffed-up appearance, because the glands are larger than normal. This closes the breathing channels of the nose and causes persistent mouth breathing. It most frequently occurs in children.

The method of treatment is to support the patient's head firmly against your chest with one hand. Exert a gentle pressure with the finger of the other hand on the identified places on each side of the nose.

Thumb rests on bridge of nose

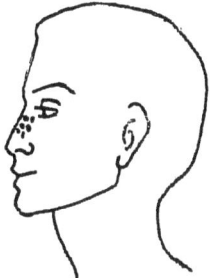

This pressure will squeeze out the surplus secretion and the breathing channel of the nose will be opened. Nature will do the rest.

The treatment may need to be given each week for 6 or 7 weeks to remold the shape of the nose if the problem has persisted for a long period of time.

Unless the eardrums have been tampered with and injured with a sharp or irritating instrument, they seldom cause deafness. The best advice is to use nothing solid to clean the ears. One drop of olive oil, no more than once a week, if necessary, will soften the wax build up and keep the ears clean.

When hearing loss begins to occur it is due to the closing or collapsing of the channels that carry air to the ear. The upper channels or tubes begin just above the eyeteeth, pass below the cheekbones to the front of the ears. The lower channels begin under the lower jawbone, forward of the area of the tonsils.

Congestion in either of these channels may be brought on by swimming, diving, extremely loud noises, by excitement or after typhoid fever or other conditions where a high temperature is involved. To restore this type of hearing loss, these channels must be cleared to allow the passage of air to the ears.

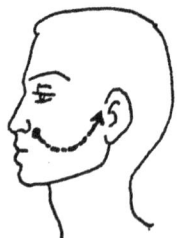

Stand behind the seated patient and place a fingertip on each side of the patient's nose, just above the eyetooth. Here you will detect indentations that are to be massaged gently. Break up any congestion to insure the passage of air through these antrum holes. Then slowly create a vacuum by drawing your fingers from these holes, underneath the cheekbone to the front of the ear. Repeat this vacuum movement 6 or 7 times.

If the lower passage is also congested, the hands are placed in the same position as for the draining movement for TONSILLITIS. The fingers create a vacuum and channel for air, from **UNDER THE LOWER JAW** to the front of the ear.

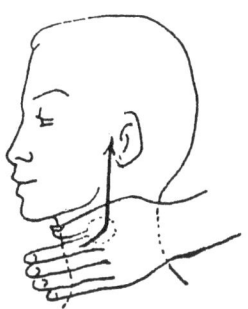

It is also possible that the tissues close to the ear have become congested. Use a gentle massage with the fingertips in front of the ear, below the ear and around the back of the ear to soften these tissues.

If the glands in the throat, especially below the ear, are swollen, they must be drained by creating a vacuum downward. Nature will complete the process.

When both upper and lower channels are open and air can pass through to the ears, the ears may be vacuumed, one at a time or both together. This part of the treatment depends on the training of the Creative Healer and the sensitivity of the patient. The vacuum treatment is helpful for dizziness and loss of equilibrium.

Remind the patient to breathe through the mouth throughout the treatment and ask that dentures be removed.

TONSILS

Tonsils are an important part of our body's defense mechanism and should be kept in a healthy condition. We naturally breathe in impurities with every breath. and one function of the tonsils is to kill any foreign elements with which they may come in contact. An abrupt change in local temperature such as a draft or chill to the throat region may permit the multiplication of germs, resulting in inflammation and swelling.

"A GERM CANNOT GROW IN NORMAL TEMPERATURE" and regardless of the cause, the treatment is to remove the heat and start the drainage. Then the swelling will subside and the tonsils will be reduced to their normal size and the body will heal itself quickly.

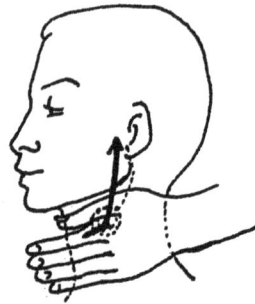

The method of treating tonsillitis is to stand behind the seated patient, use both hands, one on each side of the throat. The palms cover the hot spots in the upper throat region. Stroke gently upward and back toward the ear, bringing your fingers up to the front of the ear before returning the palms to the throat. Remember that the palm of the hand removes the heat and the fingers create a vacuum that drains the glands. The palms are cooled by the air as the hands return to the throat to pick up more heat. Continue action until all heat has been removed from the tonsil region.

Usually 3 treatments at 2 day intervals are sufficient.

STREP THROAT OR QUINSEY

The characteristic features of this kind of throat trouble are: difficulty in swallowing, and hot spots and swelling which are located mainly in the mid-region of the throat. It is a much more serious condition than tonsillitis because it may cause such inflammation that the throat becomes closed and then the patient can neither eat or drink and becomes weak.

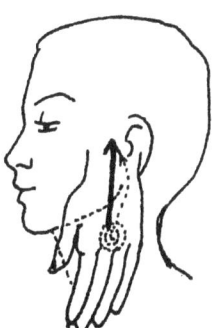

The method of removing heat and draining uses well-oiled palms which are placed on the hot spots located in the mid-region of the throat. A vacuum and drainage channel is created to the front of the ears. (The same spot as for Tonsillitis) The hands move vertically upward, the palms collecting the heat and the fingers draining the congestion from the area.

The treatment is continued at intervals, allowing the patient to lie down to rest in between, until the heat is gone and the patient can swallow a small glass of water at room temperature.

Treat every day for four days, and then as needed for complete relief.

LARYNGITIS (loss of voice)

In laryngitis, the hot spot is found just below the larynx. It is usually accompanied by the loss of voice or hoarseness because the vocal chords cannot function normally since they have been dried out by the localized heat in the voice box. The drainage movement brings the natural secretions down to wet the vocal chords and restore normal function.

To treat this condition, sit at the side of the patient so that the open palm may massage the front of the neck, downward only, from the larynx to where the chest changes its curvature. This positive massage will remove the heat and inflammation with the palm of the hand and the flow of saliva will be stimulated. The fingers and thumb come together to create a vacuum for drainage. Nature will then finish the healing in this area.

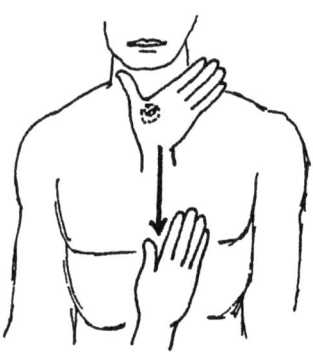

Treatment continues until all heat is removed, which may take from 15 to 20 minutes due to its accumulation in the bony structure of the chest. Several treatments may be necessary.

Loss of Voice—
(without heat or soreness)

Loss of voice may also be caused by overstraining the voice in some way. A ring of cartilage found above the voice box may become displaced thereby preventing proper functioning of the vocal chords.

Take the ring of cartilage, which is visibly protruding to the left or right side of the throat, between the thumb and forefinger of your hand. Exert a gentle pressure to center the ring. Occasionally it will make a clicking sound as it slips into place. The voice will be restored.

DRY COUGH RELIEF

White Karo syrup was recommended by Mr. Stephenson to relieve a scratchy dry throat.

The patient lies on his back with a small quantity of white Karo within reach. Place a tiny drop of syrup on his tongue. The Karo will spread and creep to wet all the dry spots for as long as he can avoid swallowing. Repeat as necessary. Avoid swallowing a spoonful of Karo as this will not help!

Feeding the Eyes

Every part of the body which has not been properly fed will show weakness. When the eyes begin to dim prematurely sufficient blood is not being delivered to keep them in their natural, healthy state. Lack of circulation to the eyes may be the beginning of cataract condition. If the eyes are properly nourished, they will be strengthened and come back to normal.

There is a contact between the back of the head and the eyes. Two oval-shaped grooves are found on the back of the head, level with the corners of the eyes.

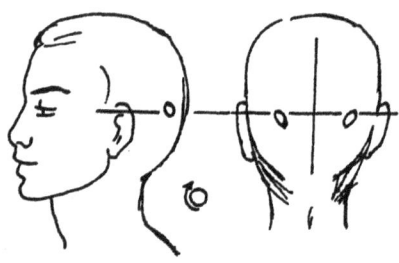

Support the patient's head with one hand. Place the thumb and middle finger of the other hand in the grooves. The grooves are easily detected as depressions unless badly obstructed, and then may still be recognized because they feel spongier than the surrounding tissue.

Massage gently with the thumb and finger in a slow, rhythmic, circular motion. The pressure is toward the eyes and up to the top of the groove. Then the thumb and finger circle downward without pressure. The feeding spots are crossed with the eyes, the right side feeding the left eye. Slight pressure on both sides at once may correct double vision.

THE EYES

Feeding the Eyes
Do not over-feed the eyes. A minute at a time is enough and do no more than fifteen minutes in any one week.

A self-treatment may be done easily with one's forefingers or thumbs (the fingers being more sensitive). Mothers can learn to treat their children.

Feeding is **never** done for inflamed eyes or when the eyelids are red or granulated with a feeling like there might be sand in the eyes. When eyes bulge as in a goiter condition, feeding is not the solution. In these cases, it is important to give the General Treatment as a preliminary to the Withdrawing Treatment.

Withdrawing From the Eyes
This treatment is given when one or both eyes are severely congested, or for simple eye strain.

There are grooves in the occipital bone beginning about 1/2 inch below the spots for feeding the eyes. The motion is reversed as the thumb and finger circle downward. Using the thumb and finger, create a vacuum over the grooves through which the congestion may be encouraged to drain.

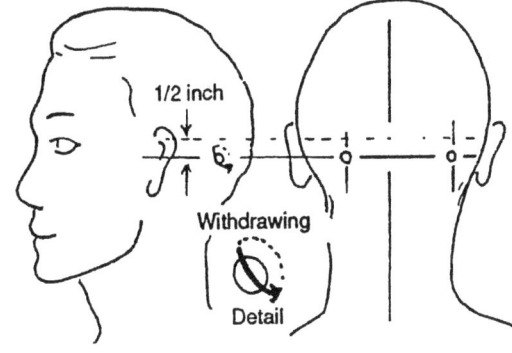

The withdrawing vacuum movement is much lighter than the feeding massage and more rapid. The withdrawing grooves are not crossed with the eyes as are the feeding spots.

The withdrawing treatment may be extended to ten or fifteen minutes when one or both eyes are severely congested.

**SELF-RELIEF FOR
TIRED OR STRAINED EYES**

Instead of rubbing tired eyes, teach yourself this treatment:

———

Locate the small grooves at the outward corners of the eyes. Place a forefinger on each groove and gently massage toward the eye. This will stimulate the secretion to the eyes and they will feel as if they have been bathed.

It is quite possible to administer all the treatments for the ears and eyes to oneself.

THE FACE

Face Lift
The tissues of the face are different than all other tissues of the body. For example, facial muscles as a whole, do not develop with use as do other muscles. In treating the face, never knead, tug or pull the tissues but gently mold them into shape as though molding clay. Any stroking of the face should be very gentle and always upward. This includes washing and drying the face and applying creams and lotions.

The massage is very gentle but with a positive intent. Lift one side of the face at a time using the palms of both hands one following another in an upward movement to the temple. This will only lift the facial tissues allowing blood and nerve life to rush in under and regenerate the skin.

It will be interesting and effective to have the patient watch the lifting in a mirror.

A part of the treatment for PAIN IN THE FACE is the lifting of the facial tissues to permit the life force to enter more quickly and fully as noted below.

Pain in the Face

The disarrangement of nerve centers and the obstruction of the life force channels to the tissues may cause excruciating pain on one side or the other of the face. A main artery that feeds the face may have moved from its position in a cavity in the bone and tissue of the lower jawbone.

The notches located on the underside of the jawbone, back toward the angle of the jaw, are easily identified. A pulse beat can be felt there, also.

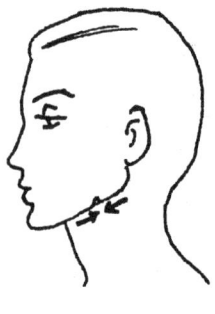

Stand behind the seated patient and draw the side of your forefinger along the under edge of the jawbone from the side of the chin into the notch. Any displacements are coaxed along and into the notch. If the slippage is behind the notch, toward the ear, draw it forward toward its natural position in the notch.

If the front of the face and the entire head is involved, a small nerve is out of place at the center of the chin. The nerve belonging to the chin can be felt only when it is out of place. It is repositioned by drawing it gently to the invisible groove in the center of the chin.

The antrum spots above the eyeteeth may be gently massaged.

THE FACE

When the obstructions have been replaced, whether left, right or center, the facial tissues must be very gently lifted but in a more exacting method than for the previously described FACE LIFT.

To lift the right side of the face, stand behind the person and rest the head against your chest. With the well-oiled palm of the right hand at the jaw level, very slowly lift the tissues of the face by the gentle suction of the palm. Carry the stroke up and as the right hand rises beyond the temple, place the first three fingers of the left hand, held horizontally, under the rising right hand, to hold the lift and bridge the time it takes the right hand to again start upward from the jaw. Reverse the above for the left side.

These problems may be caused by a prolonged dental session with the mouth open wide, a large bite into a hard apple or sleeping in a certain way for a long period of time, and there are probably other causes as well.

This treatment may be used for sagging of facial tissue as from a stroke or Bell's Palsy.

NIGHT SWEATS

The condition of excessive perspiration might follow a long illness such as tuberculosis, pneumonia, pleurisy—all of which involve some lung infection and fever. The fever could heat the sweat glands and cause them to swell and become overactive. Small shocks to the nervous system could also bring on the condition. People who are very excitable are more prone to the condition than the placid and serene type of individual.

On the back of the head near the top and about 4 inches apart and level with each other are two small depressions. Beneath these spots are nerve centers which can swell and become overactive, causing excessive sweating—often at night.

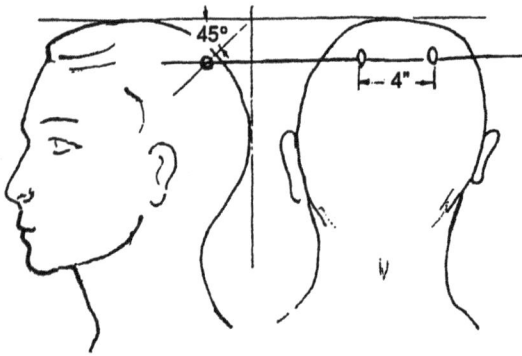

To treat, support the forehead with one hand while you exert a firm, sharp pressure with the thumb and middle finger of the other hand on the spots. The pressure is directed in and up quickly. This pressure quiets the nerve centers and the sweat glands involved. One treatment may be all that is needed, but more may be given after nature has a chance to change the programming.

HIGH BLOOD PRESSURE

The founder of Creative Healing said that there is no universal standard of blood pressure. He compared the human body to a train engine. If the engine is on a level track, it needs an even amount of pressure to meet the demand but if it has to climb a mountain, it is common sense to know that the pressure must be increased.

High blood pressure is not causatively connected with the heart. It is frequently brought on by repeated chilling of the neck. Chilling of the neck may create a coating or obstruction of the blood vessels which, in turn, impairs circulation. This causes a congestion that slows down the flow of blood returning from the head to the heart. One should become concerned when one feels dizzy or is aware of slight pains or noises in the head.

The back of the neck is a vital and delicate part of the body and obstructions there will have varied and far reaching consequences. When we consider that all the blood that reaches the head and is returned to the heart, and all the signals from the brain to all parts of the body must travel through the neck, we begin to appreciate its importance. It may be compared to a telephone exchange board where thousands of wires and inter-connected circuits interweave.

This is such an important region, that the treatment described as GENERAL TREATMENT is recommended for everyone to help restore normal functioning. It is the basis of the HIGH BLOOD PRESSURE treatment and each part is repeated in sequence several times until the pressure is reduced.

34 HIGH BLOOD PRESSURE

This treatment consists of four parts as in the General Treatment:

— carefully loosening the muscles of the upper back,

— quieting the nerves around the shoulder blades,

— thoroughly cleaning out the triangular filter areas,

— creating a vacuum downward on the sides and toward the back of the neck from the head to the filter area.

Cleaning filter area

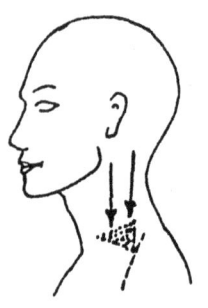

Vacuuming downward

It is given in the same sequence for the GENERAL TREATMENT but the sequence is repeated several times for a total of **20 minutes** instead of the 5 minutes of the General Treatment.

We must insure good drainage in the lymph glands (filter areas) each time, before drawing excess blood from the head by vacuuming the channels in the neck. With olive oil on the hands, the vacuuming makes a swishing sound as the movement is repeated **with contact on the downward only** part of the movement.

HIGH BLOOD PRESSURE

It is also necessary to rebuild the elasticity of the walls of the blood vessels. You will find it helpful to use a gentle massage on the sides and back of the neck, breaking up congested places. The emphasis here is also on the downward movement after the congestion is broken up.

Use two or three fingers to create a vacuum downward on the sides of the neck from the head to the filter areas.

The two dents in the occipital bone that were used in the WITHDRAWING FROM THE EYES treatment should be checked. The nerve centers, normally sheltered in these grooves, could be forced out of place by the pressure in the head, causing a stiff neck or even a headache. Use the forefingers to bring these nerve centers to their normal position.

The high blood pressure treatment lowers the blood pressure only when it is too high. If the pressure is normal or low, it will remain totally unaffected by the treatment, no matter how long it is performed.

For high blood pressure, this treatment should take 20 minutes or more and be given once a week until the pressure is lowered and stays down.

36 PAIN BETWEEN THE SHOULDERS

On the spine between the shoulder blades, there is a vital nerve and circulation center that when forced out of its position causes pain so severe that it can feel like a serious heart disturbance. In addition to a feeling like a knife going through the body, it feels impossible to take a deep breath.

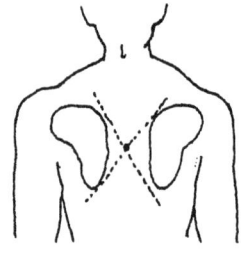

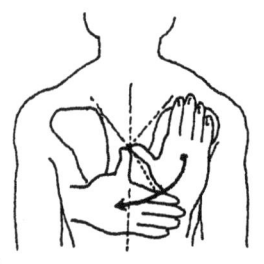

The spot is located by placing your right hand so that the fingertips are on the patient's shoulder and your thumb, held horizontal to your palm, is on the spine between two vertebrae. The space between the vertebrae may be sensitive and feel full to the touch. The spot may also be located where two lines drawn from the top to bottom of opposite shoulder blades cross the spine, as in sketch.

With the cushion of your thumb press forward on the space between the vertebrae and at the same time rotate the thumb clockwise to draw the nerve into place. Imagine the face of a clock—the thumb points to nine as you begin the twist and to twelve as you end. If the thumb goes beyond the 1/4 circle twist, the nerve could be drawn out again. This will be referred to as the "QUARTER TWIST" in many other treatments.

The thumb is a useful tool for repositioning substance between vertebrae because of the bone formation at its tip.

PAIN BETWEEN THE SHOULDERS

If the pain persists, ask the patient to take a deep breath and apply a quarter twist concurrent with exhalation and hold the shoulder back a few seconds to keep substance in place.

Stroke with the palms of both hands, one hand following the other, from the top of the spine downward to the place just treated. Three or four strokes will stimulate circulation to the area.

THE FLU SPOT

An important nerve center located in the space below the spot for Pain Between the Shoulders is useful for speeding recovery from flu or any respiratory ailment.

Both patient and operator are seated. Place the thumb to the left of the space, at arms length. This position must be held throughout the treatment, so it must be comfortable.

With the mind and the end of the thumb begin a tiny breaking-up movement, barely visible to the eye. This motion will penetrate into the center of the body where it will break up and disperse congestion.

The patient will almost immediately complain that "it hurts deep inside". This is a good sign. Ask the patient to tell you when it stops hurting because at that point the treatment is finished and nature will complete the healing process.

38 COMMON HEADACHES

This method of replacing nerve centers along the cervical vertebrae is so gentle and so easy on the patient that we are reminded of the wonderful wisdom with which the human body is created. It is equipped to do its own healing with very little help. A gentle nudge will ease the dislocated nerve center into its place.

Begin the treatment for a common or tension headache with the GENERAL TREATMENT.

Your thumb is used to detect any obstructions from the base of the neck to the skull. These obstructions may be found anywhere on either side of the cervical vertebrae.

Place your thumb on the space or the obstruction (resting your hand on the patient's shoulder). Then rotate the patient's head away from your thumb. The movement of the patient's head opens the space between the two vertebrae just enough to allow the substance to move into place. Return the head to it's original position as shown by the arrows in the illustration.

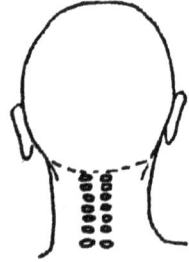 

Press obstruction while circumducting AWAY from obstruction.

EPILEPSY

Nerves that control and/or feed various organs or areas of our human body are normally smoothly embedded between two consecutive vertebrae of the entire spinal column. Epilepsy occurs when the nerve center at the base of the neck (where it joins the shoulders) is displaced to either side of the vertebrae.

If the patient falls forward during a seizure, the center is displaced to the right, if he falls backward, the displacement is to the left.

With your right hand flat on the shoulder and your thumb on the obstruction, rotate the head away from the obstruction. You will feel the nerve slip into place.

Circumducting AWAY from obstruction

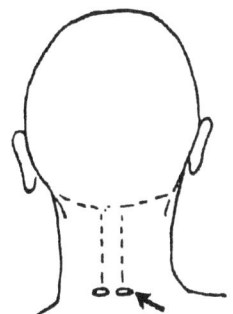

Press obstruction on RIGHT side

This illustration is for an obstruction on the right side.

Some children are born with this nerve center out of place. Sometimes it is brought on by a twist or a fall or even by turning the child upside down during play.

MIGRAINE

There is a certain nerve center on the back of the neck which controls the sense of smell. Recurrent migraine headache may be traced to a constant, day after day, inhaling of certain smells or aromas, i.e. paint, gas fumes, explosives, perfumes or any odor that is penetrating and pungent. Each person must assume responsibility to determine and eliminate aggravating odors.

When this nerve center becomes agitated it causes a swelling in a section of the brain until it is rubbing against the skull. This creates great friction and results in a violent pain at the top of the head which makes the patient feel as though the top of his head will "blow off". By replacing the displaced substance between the top vertebra and the head, the pressure is lessened and the pain disappears.

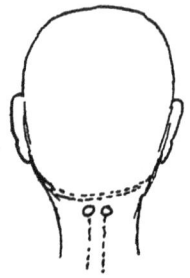

Place your right hand upright on the patient's shoulder with your thumb on the obstruction. It will be found near the skull and to the side of the vertebra—usually the right side. With your thumb pressing gently on that spot, rotate the patient's head away from your thumb. This will open the space where your thumb is pressing and allow the nerve, etc. to go back into place.

The eye cavities described in the Sinus Treatment may be massaged for relief and the General Treatment should also be given to loosen the tension and tightness in the muscles of the upper back and shoulders.

PAIN IN THE ARMS

Pain in the arms is known by many other more specific names depending on the location of the discomfort and the parts involved. The pain may be severe enough to inhibit the movement and usefulness of the arm.

In the treatments for the arm we begin to appreciate a basic truth about the functioning of our body because we can easily see the results of obstruction to the flow of "life force".

When the "life force" to the arm is obstructed, the arm will cry out to be "fed". Something needed for normal functioning is missing in this extremity.

We may or may not know exactly the specific cause of the pain in the arm, but bodies are created in such a way that we can find the obstruction and resolve the problem by using our hands in the correct and specific way for that situation.

Treatment for pain in the arm begins with the GENERAL TREATMENT with particular attention to the muscles which are parallel to the spine. These muscles have much to do with strength and energy needed in using the arms. The filter areas are cleaned to insure the flow of blood to the arm.

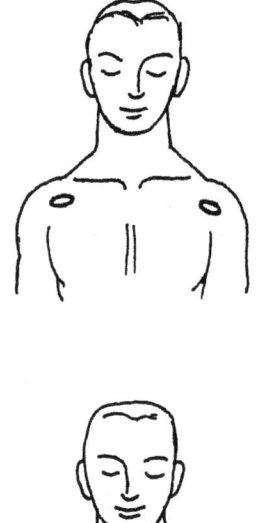

Seated behind the patient, place your hands on his shoulders with your fingers on the most prominent surface on the front side of the shoulder joint. Gently massage this area with the fingers in a breaking-up movement toward the outer-edge of the arm, to relieve the congestion you will encounter there.

If this area is too painful to be touched, then first create a vacuum down the front of the arm from shoulder to elbow to encourage the flow of blood which has been severely restricted.

Return to the congested area (a kind of knob) on the front of the shoulder and break up the congestion there until the area is no longer painful.

These two movements may be repeated. When creating the vacuum you may feel pea-like obstructions lodged in the muscle. Gently use your fingers to break up this congestion and smooth the flow of "life force" down the arm.

If, in addition to the pain, the patient has difficulty raising the arm above his head you will know that the cartilage on top of the shoulder is out of place. Your thumb is placed on the flat surface on the

PAIN IN THE ARMS

shoulder at the top of the arm. (To find it on yourself raise your elbow above your shoulder. Locate the spot that does not move when you move your arm forward and backward).

Stand at the patient's side. Form a tripod with your index and middle fingers placed on the patient's arm, pointing downward, and your thumb on the flat spot on the patient's shoulder. The patient's arm should be relaxed with the hand resting on the lap.

The pressure of the thumb is straight down, which means your elbow will probably be raised. Continue with a slow, steady pressure as the patient lowers his relaxed shoulder as far as possible.

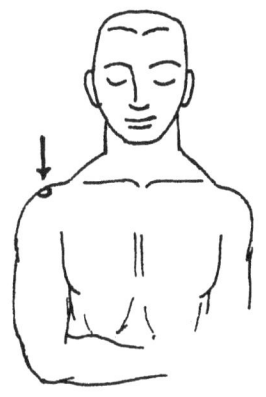

One treatment will give great relief and with all the blockages cleared nature will take over. The patient should now be able to raise the arm straight up next to the ear if the cartilage has been replaced.

The treatment may be repeated if necessary.

PAIN IN THE ELBOW

Every problem in the arm or hands is given the first two parts of the PAIN IN THE ARMS treatment to be sure this extremity is being properly "fed" the blood and nerve life.

Sometimes pain in the elbow can be quickly remedied by the following treatment:
Support the patient's elbow with one hand, while you use the thumb on the other hand to make a quick hook-like movement. The direction is indicated by the black arrow on the sketch. This movement crosses and stimulates a nerve in the elbow to restore life force.

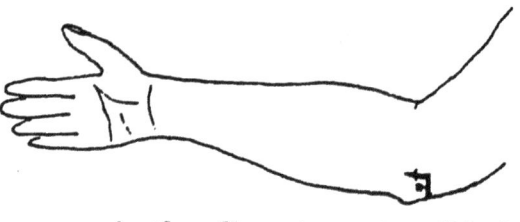

Follow this action with a vacuuming massage from the elbow through to the fingertips along the top or thumb side of the forearm.

Cartilage situated in the elbow between the upper and lower arm bones may get out of place. With the patient's arm flexed at the elbow, place your hand under the elbow and your index finger in the cavity between the upper and lower bone on the outside of the elbow. The thumb grasps the inner side to allow you to exert a gradually increasing pressure in the cavity as you slowly extend and rotate the patient's arm, ending with the palm up. The cartilage will move into place as the arm is straightened.

PAIN IN THE ELBOW

To replace cartilage in the inner side of the elbow, use the same finger and thumb hold as before. This time, with the patient's arm extended, the thumb is used to press the area in a rolling massage type pressure.

Gently massage the forearm as you look for more congested areas. This massage will bring trouble spots, like congestion or heat, to the surface where it can be easily removed with the palm.

About halfway from the wrist to elbow you may find a tender, congested area on the top of the arm. Break up the congestion with the thumb and let the palm massage through to the fingertips to restore circulation.

WRIST AND HAND CIRCULATION

Wrist
Sometimes the wrist is painful and lacks power. Displaced cartilage in the wrist may need to be repositioned.

Place the thumb on the displacement and open the space at the wrist as wide as possible. With a slight thumb pressure the cartilage will slip into its proper place.

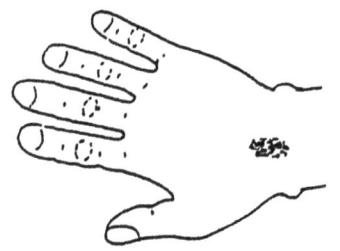

The special depression on the back of the hand at the center line of the wrist is another important filter area that must be cleaned thoroughly with a finger massage downward. This is followed by a gentle hand massage downward through to the fingertips.

When the skin on the back of the hand and the fingers is tight and white, loosen it using your thumb and fingers to gently knead it. Then stroke through to the tips of the fingers, bringing a pink color to the nails.

Finger Joints
The development of protrusions on either side of the finger joints is largely due to repeated chilling of the joints i.e. sudden changes from hot to cold water. This trouble is found more frequently in women and can be very painful. The Creative Healer may relieve the pain and teach persons to help themselves in the future.

WRIST AND HAND CIRCULATION 47

The principle of the healing motion involved is the opening of a space at each joint to allow displaced cartilage to return inside the joint where it belongs.

By flexing the finger downward and away from the protruding cartilage the space is opened. The thumb, placed on the protrusion between the top and side of the finger, presses and gradually increases the pressure until the cartilage warms and moves inside the capsule of the joint.

The finger is restored to proper articulation by extending and flexing it. Massage gently to restore circulation and nature will strengthen the joint and make it healthy.

People with swollen finger joints often exercise their fingers with the thought of preventing the stiffening of the joints. Subjecting a swollen joint to forced action will add further pressure to the capsule and increase its deterioration. As long as the swollen spots are still red and painful, the cartilage will respond to this treatment.

Cleaning the wrist filter areas and restoring finger joints for better circulation can be self-administered.

THE HEART

The Heart and Circulation
The heart is an intricate mechanism but is unbelievably rugged, often functioning against impossible odds. It fails most frequently because of the malfunctioning of other organs of the body, i.e. when circulation is blocked or digestion, kidneys, or the respiratory systems, etc. fail to function properly.

Acute Indigestion
If the person cannot lie down because of pain, suspect acute indigestion. Treat for that while the person sits upright. That much gas in the region of the heart can be dangerous.

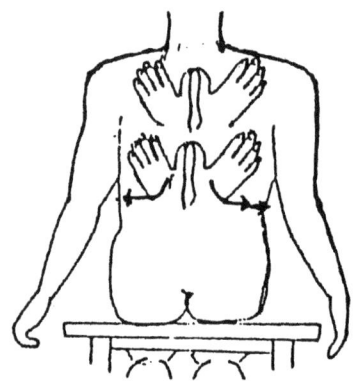

A drainage treatment similar to that in the Pneumonia Treatment is given. The drainage massage, thumbs together, hands spread across the back, begins near the shoulders. A strong steady pressure pushes the gas down and all the way around to the front of the body, towards the stomach. Work to restore the entire body to normal function.

The Basic Heart Treatment
When the heart appears in trouble, and the person is lying down, the Basic Heart Treatment is always used first. This will often take care of heart troubles.

In an emergency, the first part of the Basic Heart Treatment—the vacuum massage—could calm the

THE HEART

person and perhaps save a life. Like CPR for drowning victims, it could be taught as first aid.

In order to perform this entire treatment, you must be able to locate the 4 blood distribution centers, the #5 heart spot and the heart tube.

With the patient lying on his back on a bed, the Creative Healer is seated at the patient's right side, facing his head and able to reach comfortably across the patient's body with his right hand.

With the right palm covered with olive oil, a very gentle vacuum stroke or massage is begun where the patient's body touches the bed. The hand stroke is a gentle arc from an almost horizontal position over the ribs on the patient's left side. The wrist turns the hand so that the fingertip passes through the #5 heart spot. The palm is kept in contact with the body throughout the stroke.

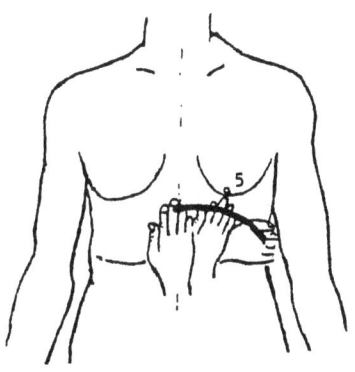

The continuing stroke brings the palm across the heart tube to create a vacuum and the stroke terminates when the palm has crossed the center line of the body. Done correctly the hand will be vertical as the stroke ends.

The whole massage is unhurried and gentle with no

pressure. The positive, even, repetitive and calming stroke of the hand creates the drainage vacuum. This massage is continued for four minutes.

This part of the treatment alone may bring such relief that the patient will take an involuntary deep, relaxing breath. This is a sign that the massage has been helpful in relieving a distressed heart and nature will take over the healing process.

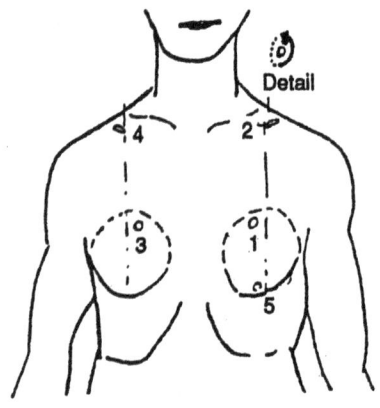

The second part of the heart treatment is done with the pad of the Creative Healer's index finger on heart spots #1, 3, and 5. Spots #2 and 4, being more oval in shape, utilize the index and middle fingers for #2 and the middle and third finger for #4. The gentle, circular movement is counter-clockwise. A delicate vacuum is accomplished during the breaking up movement by lightening the finger contact in the upward arc of the tiny circle.

The heart spots are felt as small cavities between the bones. Because the heart delivers the blood, spots 1-2-3-4 are identified as distribution centers. In these junctions are glands that function as filters and regulate the flow of blood. The very gentle, counterclockwise, finger massage may relieve pressure by breaking up any obstructions at these junctures. Perform the massage at spots 1 through 5 in numerical sequence.

THE HEART

The #5 spot is a more pronounced hollow than the four other spots and affects the blood entering the heart. Any material broken up at the first four spots is automatically channeled to the fifth spot and from there it is drawn, along with any foreign material present, into the stomach through the heart tube.

Whenever you are treating any of these spots do use a gentle pressure. This is one instance when it is much better to do too little than to do too much, because as soon as you have started the treatment, nature immediately goes to work.

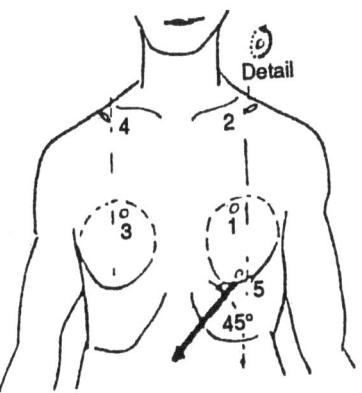

The third part of the heart treatment is concerned with the tube that lies at a 45 degree angle downward and to the center of the body from the #5 spot. This tube is protected (as are other vital spots) as it is sheltered in one of those little cavities. You must experience the truth of its existence as you massage with your hand over the rib cage from the left toward the center, as described in the first movement. You may feel or even hear something flow through this tube.

Its presence from an orthodox point of view cannot be proven as yet, but as you continue to give treatments, you will be convinced of its existence and its importance.

We have already discussed one way of creating a vacuum in the heart tube—the safest way. It is the massage stroke with which you began the treatment. When you have touched all the heart spots, return to this massage until a deep breath gives nature's signal to stop.

Repeat all three parts as needed.

Leaking Heart
In the explanation of the cause and treatment for a leaking heart we gain insight and understanding of how the basic heart treatment relieves pressure on the heart. The functioning of the heart is compared to that of a pump.

A leak inside a pump would be caused by an obstruction at the delivery end of the pump. This obstruction would cause a back pressure which would then force something to give way inside. If the pump is to continue to function, there must be some relief mechanism.

The same is true of the heart which pumps the blood. The obstruction on the delivery side of the heart (above the heart) would cause a back pressure that would force a weak blood vessel inside the heart to leak.

The obstruction would be in the blood stream above the heart in one of those 4 distributing centers—the spots which we identify as 1-2-3-4. By treating each one of these spots you can remove the obstruction from whichever one may be sore or painful. With this release a natural action takes place in the

THE HEART

heart. The leak is no longer needed. Nature then steps in and closes the vessel that had been forced to leak because of the pressure.

After removing the obstruction above the heart, always remove any congestion in the #5 heart spot in the same way. Finish the treatment with the drainage massage. The BASIC HEART TREATMENT solves many heart problems.

Regulating a Fast or Slow Heart
A fast heart may be caused by the heart tube being too far up toward the head from its normal position, while a slow heart is caused by the tube being too far down. In either case the quantity of air being supplied to the heart changes—the more air, the heart speeds up; not enough air, it slows down. The Basic Heart Treatment is given first for all heart problems.

When the heart beats too fast all other causes for fast heart must be checked out before regulating the heart tube. This would include the spot on the back described in the INWARD GOITER TREATMENT. It is also a relief mechanism connected with the heart. The double vacuum of the inward goiter treatment might be needed to restore adequate lubrication to the heart.

As a last resort we proceed to move the heart tube to its correct position—an exact 45 degree angle from the #5 heart spot to the center of the body.

With utmost care you may treat by placing your thumb one half inch **ABOVE** the normal position of the tube at the edge of the rib in the soft tissue. Use the edge of the thumb in a gentle but positive movement that carries it exactly to the 45 degree line. One movement regulates a fast heart.

Regulating a Slow Heart
When the heart tube has been displaced too far downward the heart cannot get sufficient air. Consequently it gets tired and has to take longer rests between beats. So, with the heart taking in insufficient air—the result is a slow heart.

This condition is treated in the same way except that the tube is **BELOW** its normal position. Locate the 45 degree angle with the thumb. The hand always lies gently, flat, and horizontal to the center line of the body when working with the heart tube. The thumb is now placed 1/2 inch below the 45 degree line (close to the hand). Then move the thumb upward to the line. This movement may be repeated to bring the heartbeat to normal speed.

Heart Murmur
After the BASIC HEART TREATMENT is given, a double vacuum is created on the front of the neck and chest as in INWARD GOITER to bring the oil or secretion which comes from the glands in the front of the neck to lubricate the heart through the #1 heart spot. It is like oiling an engine to keep it running smoothly. A stoppage of this secretion could be the cause of a heart murmur.

We may wonder what caused this otherwise normal flow of oil to the heart to be interrupted or stopped.

THE HEART

It is not unreasonable to suspect that a high fever from some childhood illness—as for instance rheumatic fever—might have caused this oil to burn out.

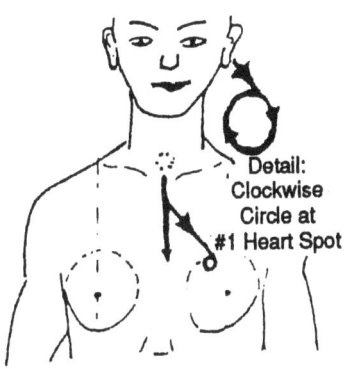

Detail: Clockwise Circle at #1 Heart Spot

Whatever the cause it can usually be corrected by distributing the lubricating secretion to the #1 heart spot in a clockwise circular movement as described in the INWARD GOITER treatment.

The importance of the thyroid gland is its regulatory function. Whether the problem is an over or under activity, it can be helped by creating this same vacuum at the base of the neck.

INWARD GOITER

Contrary to the accepted concept of the thyroid as a ductless gland, three ducts or channels issue from it: two from its outer portion and one from the interior of the thyroid.

The secretion from the interior is a fluid that acts as an oil to "lubricate" the heart. Inward goiter is an accumulation of the secretion that has congealed when the duct that carries it toward the heart is dammed up.

As the secretion congeals it causes the gland to swell. The muscles behind the eyes are fed too much secretion (making the eyes appear to protrude). Since the oil does not reach the heart, that organ speeds up and the patient becomes very nervous.

The Creative Healer is seated behind the patient with the fingers of his left hand on the left shoulder of the patient to monitor the pulse beat in the neck.

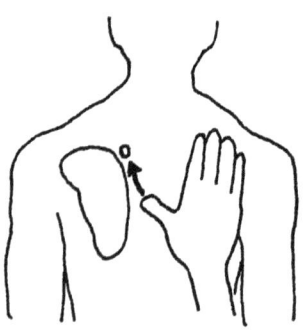

The drawing depicts one way to locate the congested heart spot. A second method is to place the oiled palm of the right hand between the spine and the left shoulder blade, you will locate the spot by its high temperature.

Remove the congestion from this spot with the cushion of the thumb in a small, gentle clockwise circular

INWARD GOITER

massage. It will soon be noticed that the heart has slowed and the nervous vibrations have disappeared.

As in the sketch, stroke with the palms to distribute into the circulation what has been broken up at the spot, without touching the spot again.

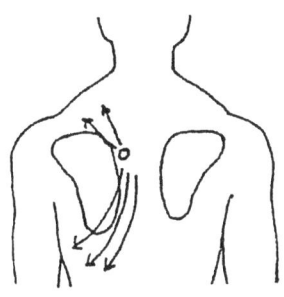

The next step is to stand at the front and side of the patient where the hand may operate freely at the illustrated line to create a vacuum. This is done with three fingers and plenty of olive oil. If the first and third fingers are held a bit in front of the middle finger, a double vacuum will be created as they are repeatedly moved downward from beneath the larynx for a length of 3 or 4 inches in each stroke.

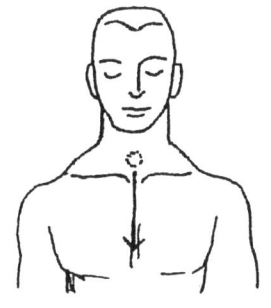

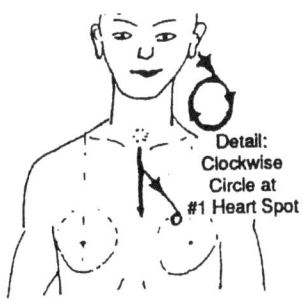

Detail: Clockwise Circle at #1 Heart Spot

This stroking must be continued for seven minutes to soften and establish the drainage of the secretion. During that time direct your fingers gently 3 or 4 times to the #1 heart spot with a **CLOCKWISE** circular movement as described in HEART MURMUR Treatment.

The third part of this treatment will be on the back of the head where the thumb and forefinger create a vacuum to withdraw pressure from the eyes. These spots are one-half inch below the eye feeding spots and are detailed in WITHDRAWING FROM THE EYES.

This entire treatment should be given once a week for seven weeks.

HIGH AND SHORT BREATHING 59

A gasp for air as the result of sudden shock, a jump into cold water, or an accident may cause high and short breathing. It may also develop as a bad breathing habit through not using the diaphragm completely. Whatever the cause, the lungs cannot exhale completely and the chest is forced to heave with each breath.

Give the full BASIC HEART TREATMENT with emphasis on the stroking massage. Both sides of the chest over the ribs should be massaged to loosen tightness in that area. Next, we create a vacuum in the breathing tube to draw out excess air from the pleural cavity. See sketch.

The breathing tube is envisioned as a passage leading from the pleural cavity into the stomach. It lies on the center line of the body and it helps maintain normal breathing.

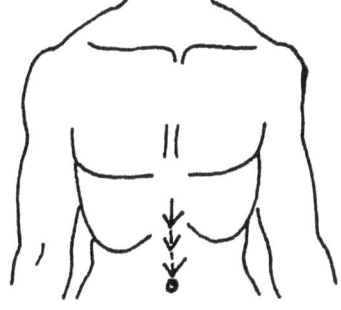

The thumb is drawn lengthwise from the breastbone down the exact center line of the body, for three or four inches, repeatedly, with an occasional stroke to the navel.

This action will not only evacuate the pleural area but will clean out the tube and relieve the tension at a most important nerve center—the solar plexus.

HIGH AND SHORT BREATHING

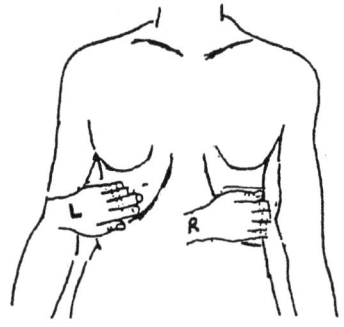

When the patient takes a deep breath, place your hands completely on the ribs below the sternum, as illustrated in the accompanying sketch. On the next exhalation, assist the lungs to empty.

With the hands distributing an even pressure, positively, yet smoothly, pull the ribs in and downward toward the spine and feet. This will force excess air from the lungs, will loosen the tightness on the ribs and will bring the chest down to its normal position.

There are many other uses for the vacuuming treatment at the center of the body as you will discover. We often put our hand over this area involuntarily. This is a treatment you can give yourself for acid stomach, hiccough, etc.

DIAPHRAGMATIC BREATHING

While walking, teach yourself to breathe diaphragmatically (normal breathing). Inhale for 6 steps, hold for 4 steps and exhale completely during 4 steps, then allow the lungs to relax 4 steps. Repeat.

TIGHT CLOTHING

When you wear elastic waistbands, belts, undergarments, stockings or any article of clothing be sure it is not too tight.

Normal clothing marks should disappear within 5 minutes after undressing. Problems result if the body is being restricted too much.

When the flow of action of the many vital functions of the organs and muscles is cut off, everything tends to sag into the floor of the pelvis, causing problems.

The results of these restrictions may cause nausea, dysfunctioning of the digestive and eliminations tracts, a lack of energy or the person may simply not feel up to par.

These troubles will continue until the person recognizes his or her responsibility to keep the body unrestricted to enable the abdominal muscles to regain their tone.

The habit of sitting with arms crossed and resting on the abdomen tends also to press everything into the floor of the pelvis.

Be aware of these things and help yourself!

62 PNEUMONIA OR LUNG CONGESTION

The treatment for all congestion in the lungs is to massage with the intention of drawing out the fever. The pneumonia patient must be kept in bed.

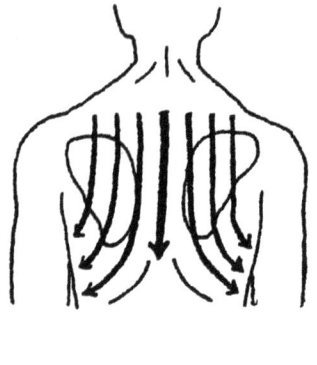

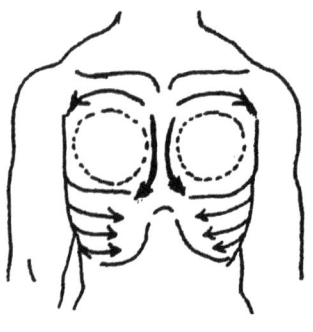

Using plenty of olive oil, massage the chest, then turn the patient over and massage the back in the same way. The massage is done with a double stroke to the same area, one hand following the path of the other, quickly and without pressure.

Continue the treatment (which may take thirty to forty minutes) until the patient's body temperature feels normal to your hands.

Use drainage movement (page 48 illustration) to redirect erratic circulation.

USE OF MILK
Anyone who is recovering from all forms of lung and head congestion should avoid milk and milk products.

VITAMIN D
Chest conditions that linger and weaken the person may be helped by the use of Vitamin D as found in cod liver oil.

ASTHMA

Asthma is a condition associated with breathing difficulty and it might begin with a draft or a chill. It could come from shock or a deformity of the upper part of the body. However, it is more likely associated with various kinds of dust: coal, iron, rock, sand or any small particles which may be inhaled through the nose.

Whatever the cause, the particles accumulate in the lungs, clogging the pores and putting so much weight on the lungs that they are unable to expand or contract normally.

Notice that the body of an asthmatic person feels cold and somewhat clammy to the touch, particularly in the lower region of the lungs. This area is below normal temperature and there is usually a cough that is tiring but brings up nothing.

The first intent of the Creative Healer is to bring these colder areas to normal temperature. The patient is seated, if possible, and so is the Creative Healer. With a little oil on the palms a friction massage to bring warmth is given over the upper back and the chest. Working fairly rapidly, one hand follows the other in full length double strokes with a firm pressure. Straight elbows will create the additional pressure needed.with same movements as shown in page 62 illustration.

When the heat warms the mucous, the patient is able to cough productively. The more mucous raised the more space is cleared for breathing capacity. The accumulation in the lung sacs can only be eliminated by expectoration.

The drainage movement is similar to the drainage movement for the PNEUMONIA TREATMENT. However, for asthma the hands are placed higher up on the back and the movement is down and diagonally to the front and center of the body covering the entire lung area.

Then clean out and drain the pleural cavity through the Breathing Tube on the front of the body as described in HIGH AND SHORT BREATHING Treatment.

Notice the position of the ribs. If they flare outward, use the rib treatment in HIGH AND SHORT BREATHING to carefully bring the ribs closer together.

In some cases the patient should wear a five inch band to bind the ribs in position and force the use of the diaphragm in breathing. See Box below.

BINDER FOR WEIGHT LOSS
The five inch binder is also useful for other conditions. People who want to lose weight should be reminded that the first fat to be lost is that which cushions the vital organs. Bringing the ribs in will insure the protection of these organs.

BINDER FOR BABIES
In times past a binder was used on new babies to insure correct breathing and to help drain the pleural region after birthing.

BINDERS FOR NEW MOTHERS
New mothers would regain their slim waists if the ribs were brought in and banded snugly but comfortably.

KIDNEYS

The kidneys act as the filter of the blood stream. If they are not fed enough nerve life, they may be forced to operate at above normal body temperature. In this condition they will not be able to cleanse the blood stream as they should.

Nerve life is fed to the kidneys from the "kidney spot"—a space between two vertebrae on the spine. A displacement of substance or a contraction in the surrounding region will affect the nerve center which governs the flow of nerve life to the kidneys. The area may be sensitive.

The patient should be sitting upright so that gravity will work in the healing process. Seated behind the patient, place the palms of your hands in the space above the hips on the back over the kidneys. With wrists together raise the right thumb to locate the "kidney spot" between two vertebrae.

The quarter circle twist is performed by the thumb here and also in the space above and the space below the identified space. This movement can be repeated both to the left and to the right of the space between each vertebra to reposition the substance or relieve the contraction.

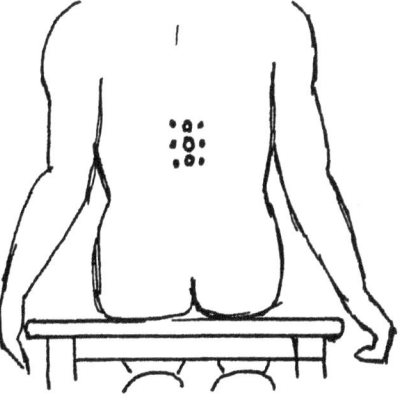

KIDNEYS

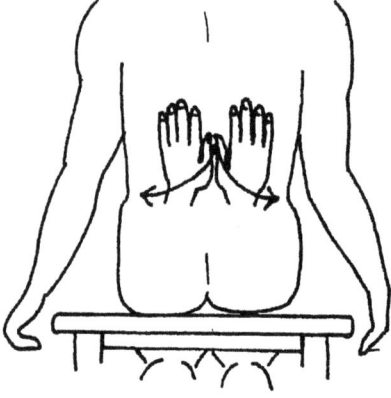

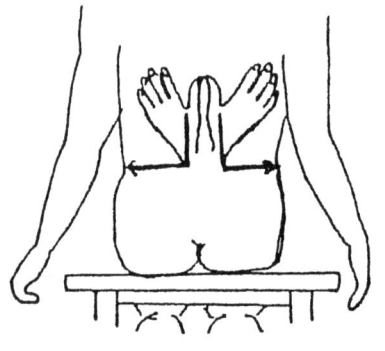

Continue the treatment by gently massaging diagonally downward from these nerve centers to the kidneys with the palms of the hands. The natural vacuum in the palms of the hands will remove any heat that is brought to the surface of the skin. The treatment is **VERY GENTLE** with the positive thought of bringing in new "life force" and action to the kidneys.

Finish the treatment by placing the length of the thumbs together at center back and spreading the hands across the back of the patient. Bring the hands with a positive movement downward until the fingertips are just below the ribcage. Then separate the hands with thumbs following the fingers to each side of the body thereby creating a double drainage vacuum.

Problems with kidneys could be caused by an injury or by digestive disorders in the stomach, pancreas, liver, or even a heart condition. A DIGESTIVE TUNE UP is recommended. On the other hand, kidneys that are in trouble can seep a poison into the sciatic nerve and cause a chronic low back pain.

GENERAL LOCATIONS FOR CREATIVE HEALING APPLICATIONS ON THE LOWER BACK

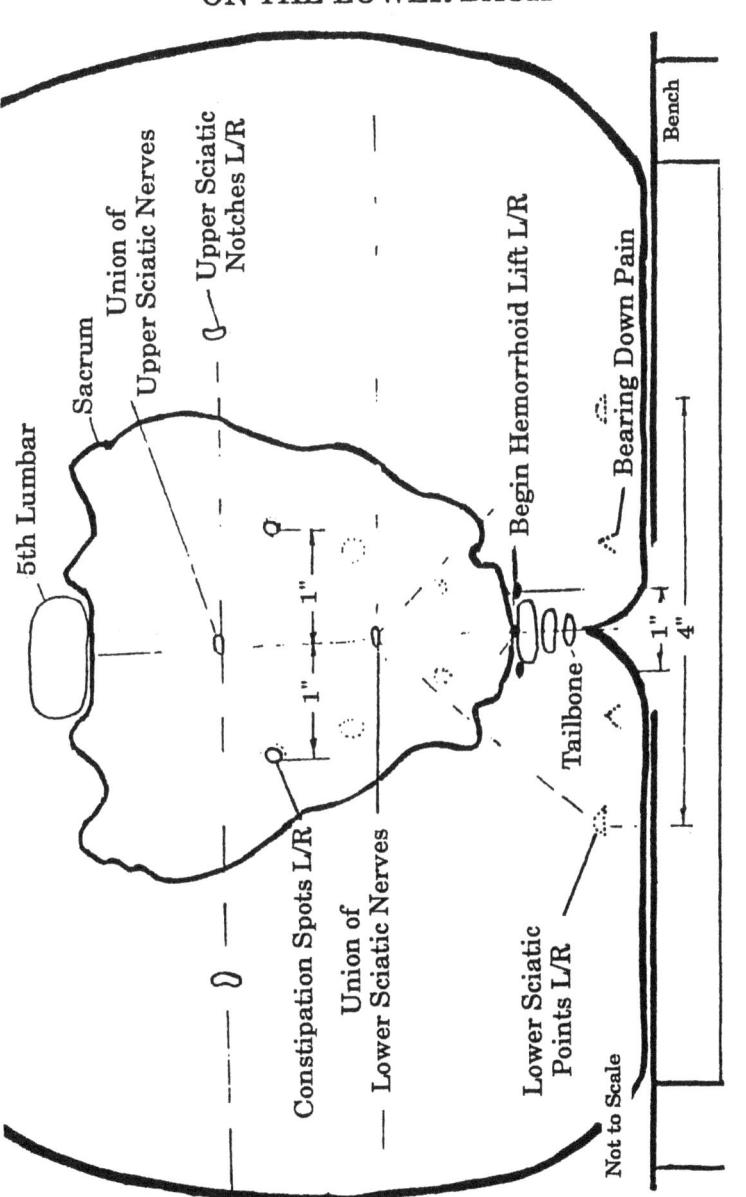

Many people suffer from a painful condition in the lower part of the back and legs never knowing that something can be done to alleviate the problem. The causes are many: accidents, sprain, a twist of the body, etc. The debilitating effects may be corrected by restoring the flow of nerve life that has been impaired, whatever the specific cause may have been. The pelvic girdle is a pivot for the entire body, functioning when standing, walking, sitting, turning, etc. and the importance of these treatments to the lower back should not be minimized.

Lower Sciatic Nerve
The patient is seated on a bench in an upright position, the Creative Healer is seated behind him. With the thumbs about one inch apart on each side of the spine at the cleavage, rest your elbows on your knees. By slowly drawing your knees together the thumbs will be forced upward in a slow steady movement, coming together where the nerve is likely to be displaced.

If the patient is in much pain, use only a little pressure and alternate with an upward massage that will draw out congestion and inflammation. This will ease the pressure on the nerve and the patient will be more comfortable. Then using the quarter twist at the spine on the painful side or in the middle, release the pinch by replacing the nerve upward.

Using the fingers of both hands simultaneously, stroke over the lower nerve paths. Begin where the buttocks join the bench near the tailbone and follow the nerve channel around to the joints of the hips.

SCIATICA

(follow diagram) Use the breaking up movement if there is soreness at the hip joint.

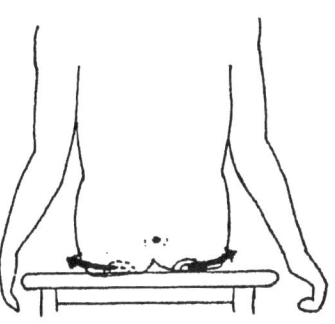

Follow the nerve path down the leg to the back of the thigh. The patient may not be aware of any trouble here because if these muscles are contracted or in spasm the pain would be felt in the lower back.

With the patient lying face down, release these muscular contractions by massaging with an upward motion under the buttocks until the tissues become softer and the pain eases. The contractions disappear as the blood circulation and nerve energy penetrate the muscles.

Now, with the patient lying on his side, the nerve path may be traced down the outside of the leg. The palm used in a gentle massage will quickly detect trouble, i.e. muscular contractions or inflammation that is present. Redness or heat will show up immediately.

Next, the glands of the ankle are massaged, as the patient lies on his back. To insure good circulation both to the feet and also to the muscles of the leg, it is necessary to clean out the filter area. See Ankle Filter Treatment.

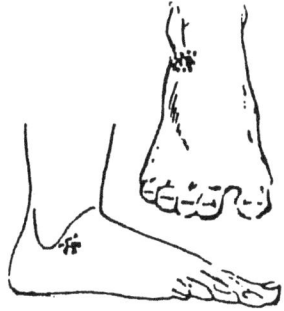

It is often useful at this point to return and treat again the lower back with the thumb twist at the side of the spine. the patient sitting upright, of course.

Upper Sciatic Nerve

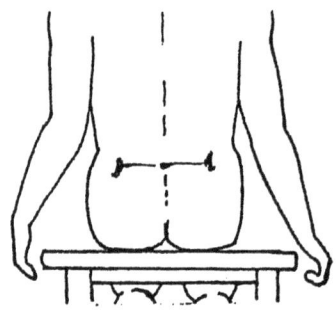

Find the cavities on each side of the lower back as shown in the sketch. Trace a straight line from the cavities to the spine to locate the upper sciatic nerves. The juncture of the two upper sciatic nerves is lifted into its groove in the bone and tissue by the quarter twist.

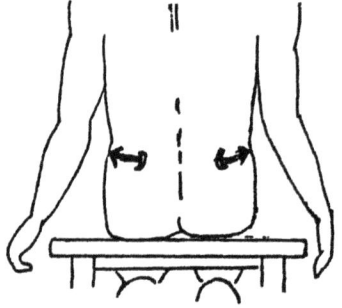

To replace the nerve on the right or left side, again use the thumb in the quarter twist, pressing gently toward the spine and up as in your mind you see it move up into its groove.

Return to the notches with a circular breaking up movement with the fingers of both hands and then stroke in a straight line around the hip, following the nerve path through the groove on the front edge of the hipbones. Repeat this movement several times.

SCIATICA

The upper sciatic nerve passes downward from the hip through the groin and on the inside of each leg to the feet. Again, the pain is followed and relieved in the entire leg as described in the LOWER SCIATICA treatment. Since this nerve always sags downward, to lift it massage lightly UPWARD from the knee to the groin.

CONSTIPATION

Constipation is the result of the contents of the bowel becoming hard and dry. When the body is functioning correctly an adequate mucous secretion is emitted by certain glands that keep the bowel moving smoothly.

The glands lie about an inch on each side of the center back and are usually identifiable as dimples on the sacrum. They have a spongy feeling. This treatment stimulates these glands so that they will emit the needed amount of mucous secretion.

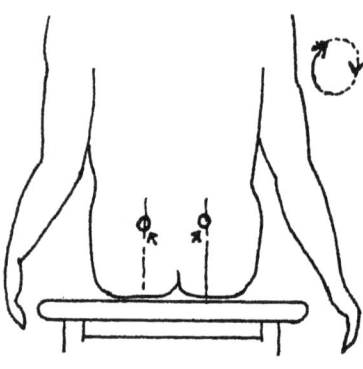

The Creative Healer sits behind the seated patient. The thumbs are placed just below the constipation spots, the fingers on the buttocks of the patient. By placing the elbows on the knees, and moving the legs toward and away from each other, the thumbs will move in a circular motion. The quite rapid motion of the knees allows the thumbs to stimulate the glands to manufacture and release their secretion into the rectum.

The treatment should continue for six or seven minutes.

Babies and little children may be helped as they lie on their stomach. Use the fingertips gently on each side of the spine in only 3 or 4 upward strokes. Teach mothers how to treat for constipation.

HEMORRHOIDS

Sitting or standing too long without a position change, sitting on a cold surface or unreasonable pressure to move the bowels are activities that may cause hemorrhoids. The rectal muscles lose strength when the natural feed is cut off or interrupted for too long a time.

When the muscles that support the rectum weaken and sag, they cause hemorrhoids. The sagging causes blood vessels to swell and penetrate into the rectum. They may protrude beyond the anus and rupture, producing bright red blood.

An effective treatment must feed and strengthen the rectal muscles and restore the rectum to its proper position. The inner tissues respond to the combination of the lifting of the tissue on the outside of the sacrum and the Creative Healer's thoughts that KNOW the lifting is also taking place inside.

The patient is seated. The Creative Healer, seated behind the patient, places his thumbs about an inch apart on each side of the spine. The elbows are on the knees.(See diagram)

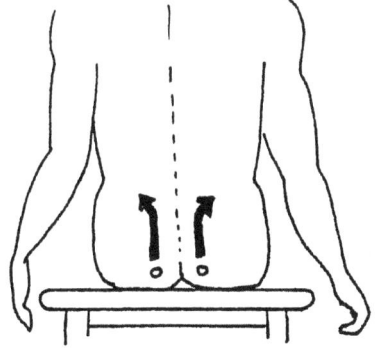

The knees are gradually moved together and thus force the thumbs upward in a very slow and steady movement that moves the tissues toward the top of the sacrum.

The patient is sitting quietly, so that the pressure remains constant with the intent that **everything that passes under the thumbs is lifted.** Six or seven "lifts" are given in one treatment. An upward only massage may be interspersed to relieve the thumbs and increase circulation to that entire part of the body.

A treatment a week for four or five weeks may be needed. Be advised that toilet paper should not be used because tiny wood fibers in the paper adhere to and embed in the mucous membranes, causing more problems. A soft cloth or sponge may be used instead until healing is complete.

Self treatment is not easy but may be done by placing the middle fingers, supported by the index fingers of both hands, at the base of the spine and steadied by placing the thumbs on the buttocks as the lifts are made.

BOWEL CONSCIOUSNESS

The bowel is susceptible to induced habits. It can be consciously 'trained' by establishing one or two times every day when the bowel is given time to empty. Allow sufficient time for this natural action—the bowel will respond!

BEARING DOWN PAIN

This pain is not evident when sitting or standing, but the strain is very severe when attempting to stand up from a sitting position or to sit down from a standing position. One or both of two nerve centers located on each side of the spine have been forced out of position. Their normal position being in little cavities or dents in the bone on which the body rests when sitting.

The tip of the forefinger (nail cut short) is placed on the cavity below the outer edge of the tailbone. The fingertip lifts the tissue into the highest point of an inverted V-shaped notch between the sacrum and the tailbone. It will be necessary to place elbow on knee for sufficient pressure to push the nerve up into place.

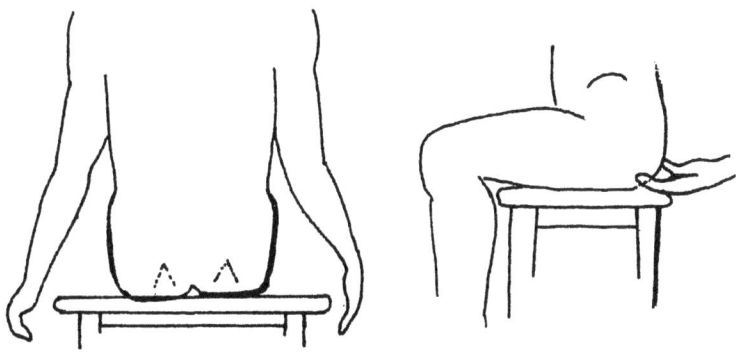

Slow, steady pressure will relax the muscles and allow the fingertip to penetrate to the highest point of the notch where the nerve is replaced. One treatment is sufficient.

ABDOMINAL MASSAGE

In treating the organs of the digestive tract, use a massage to the abdominal area first. THE ONLY EXCEPTION IS WHEN THERE IS HEAT IN THE ABDOMEN. Heat is **ALWAYS** removed before giving this treatment.

The patient should be reminded not to eat before a digestive treatment and should be asked to empty the bladder before beginning the treatment.

There are 3 parts to the Abdominal Massage. Use olive oil.

Begin at the lower abdomen on the left side, along the descending colon. The finger tips begin the upward stroke and as they move upward the entire hand including the palm, follows in contact with the body. The stroke continues to the base of the ribs.

The second movement is the same but on the right side of the abdomen along the ascending colon.

The third stroke is in the center. Place your open hand just above the pelvic bone and as the hand moves up, the palm will be in contact. All these motions are in an upward direction only. The use of the palm is stressed because of its natural vacuum and its potential healing power.

LIVER

The liver is the largest gland of the body. Located on the right side, beneath the ribs, its upper surface fits against the under surface of the diaphragm. Its under surface fits over the right kidney.

The natural function of the liver is to manufacture bile and purify the blood. It is important that the delivery end of this organ is kept fully operable. If the bile backs up and the liver becomes sluggish, the entire digestive system is affected.

This easy-to-give treatment may also be self administered. This method of cleaning the bile duct and bringing the liver into action is very effective. Whenever a vacuum is created in the human body it must be filled immediately. "Nature abhors a vacuum."

The patient is lying down with the Creative Healer seated at his right side. The thumb is used to find the first notch on the upswing of the lowest rib on the right side. The hand is placed flat on the body 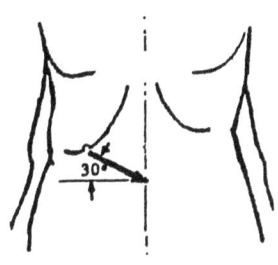 so that the length of the thumb is free to create a vacuum. The thumb begins on the rib above the notch and glides over a 30 degree angle to the center line of the body. When the vacuum has been established you may hear or feel a flow under your thumb.

Guard against overtreating by remembering that you begin the process of healing, then nature takes over and continues the work. Always use olive oil.

GALL BLADDER

The gall bladder could be called the reservoir for bile generated by the liver. So it is understandable that its functioning is dependent upon the liver. This tells us that if the gall bladder needs help, the liver also needs attention. Discomfort or hardness in that area may be noticed after eating chocolate, ice cream or drinking milk. If this organ is functioning in a healthy way, stones will not develop.

The gall notch is located by tracing along the lower edge of the ribs, upward from the liver notch to the second notch on the right side of the body. Under this notch lies the nerve center controlling the gall bladder.

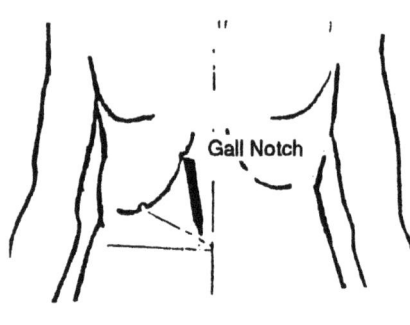

The method of treatment is similar to that of the LIVER. A vacuum is created with the thumb in a long stroke of four or five inches, almost parallel to the center line. It meets the path of the liver duct.

Pain at the junction of the gall and liver ducts is eliminated by directing a vacuum stroke through the intersection of the two ducts to move the obstruction out.

PANCREAS

The pancreas is a large, elongated gland or organ which lies behind the stomach. It performs a very necessary digestive function by secreting a fluid which mixes with the food in the duodenum. An overactive pancreas could bring on acid stomach and heartburn.

It also secretes the hormone insulin. If the pancreas begins to dry out, the lack of insulin will lead to diabetes. A relentless, dull ache beneath the ribs in front on the left side, an unquenchable thirst, and drowsiness are indications of a drying out pancreas.

The principle of creating a vacuum is used in treating this gland. Place three fingers of the right hand just under the ribs on the patient's left side as he lies on his back. The movement begins where the fingertips touch the bed and continues to the front of the body. To more easily 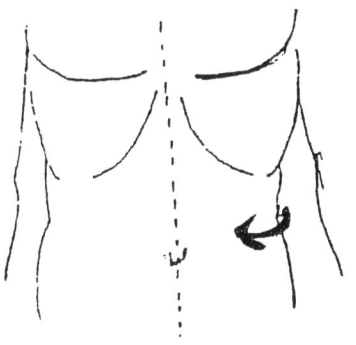 sustain this long stroke, rest the thumb lightly on the patient's ribs and use the wrist to roll the forearm and hand, in a short flipping movement, while the fingers remain straight. Repeat to establish the vacuum.

Once or twice during the vacuuming movement, glide the hand to the pit of the stomach to check the temperature. If there is trouble the stomach will feel below normal temperature. The treatment may vary from 5 to 20 minutes depending on the need and warmth of the stomach. The objective is to bring the stomach to normal temperature.

The pancreas is then **FED** on the right side of the body. Here, the length of the thumb is used along the bottom of the ribs, following them from where they touch the bed to halfway between the liver and gall notches. The stroke is a continuous one with a positive feeding pressure. The time spent on feeding is about 40 percent of the time spent creating a vacuum on the left side. For example: 10 minutes vacuum and 4 minutes feeding.

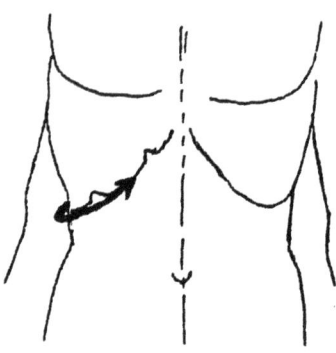

The vacuum treatment cleans out and enlivens the pancreas and the feeding treatment strengthens and brings in increased nourishment. Feeding the pancreas also helps clean out liver wastes.

ENO FRUIT SALTS

Mr. Stephenson recommended ENO, a natural, lemon flavored, effervescing fruit salts, to relieve stomach gas, distress from eating the wrong or too much food, acute indigestion and to calm the solar plexus. Add 1/2 to 3/4 teaspoon of Eno to 1/2 glass of warm water. Drink while fizzing. Eno is well known in England, Stephenson's birthplace, but it can be found in large drug stores everywhere.

SPLEEN

The spleen is a bean-shaped organ situated directly beneath the diaphragm, behind and to the left of the stomach. Its concave side is toward the tail of the pancreas. It is shrouded by the lower ribs on the left side of the body. If the spleen is congested, the region of the body over it will be sensitive and sometimes painful to the lightest touch. The patient may complain of sore ribs. The region will often be warm to the touch.

To decongest the spleen, apply a vacuum movement similar to that in the BASIC HEART TREATMENT.

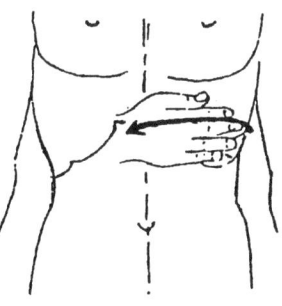

The patient lies on his back, the creative healer sits at his right side. The vacuum stroke begins with the palm centered over the region of the spleen. (The hot spot for the spleen is found almost under the body, so the palm must start very low toward the bed in such cases.) Stroke over the rib cage as illustrated, continuing across the median line of the body.

This drawing action is continued about 20 minutes. Within this time there may be a release of congestion beneath the area of the stroking. This action may cause the patient to shake or ask for a drink of water. All effects will usually disappear within 5 minutes—the length of time required by the blood stream to absorb the material released.

Treat once a week until congestion is relieved.

In times past our food was grown without contaminants and preserved without additives. We are learning to appreciate the role that good food plays in our lives.

To fill the stomach with anything in excess, such as alcohol, soft drinks, meat or sweets, is to require the organs to do an impossible task and sooner or later one or more will be affected and affect the functioning of other parts of the body. We must learn to treasure this remarkable, computer-like instrument we call our body and teach our children to respect its faithful and high-level functioning.

With that in mind, Mr. Stephenson felt that the Creative Healing Treatments for all the digestive organs when given together when there is no problem would promote good maintenance of the body. This periodic checkup is called*, a DIGESTIVE TUNE-UP. As any automobile owner realizes, a "tune-up" is important to keep a car running smoothly. Just so, the Digestive Tune-up could be used to prevent problems from developing and keep things running smoothly in the body.

A Digestive Tune-up is a good thing any time for anyone. It begins with the abdominal massage. The complete tune-up includes treatments for LIVER, GALL BLADDER, PANCREAS and HEART. All Creative Healing Treatments are so gentle they could never do anything but good—it is their specificity that makes them helpful.

*Editor's contribution

ULCERATED STOMACH

The stomach is a muscular organ that is in action all the time and this is an important factor in understanding how an ulcer develops. Friction develops when the muscular wall comes in contact with hot acidic contents through a weak place in the lining of the stomach. Raw muscles rubbing together, cause a sore spot that festers and ulcerates.

The objective of the Creative Healing treatment is to locate the sore spot, separate the muscles from rubbing on each other long enough to allow circulation to be restored. This removes the friction and allows nature to heal the area.

Gently massage the area to draw the heat of the ulcer to the surface. A red spot will appear to indicate the location and size of the ulcer.

Place your hands as indicated by the sketch and massage **AWAY FROM** the ulcer with the lower hand only. The other hand is holding the flesh above the ulcer to keep it from moving. In so doing, you are separating the muscular folds of the stomach and allowing the natural juices to flow. With the friction removed even briefly, nature is ready to begin the healing process.

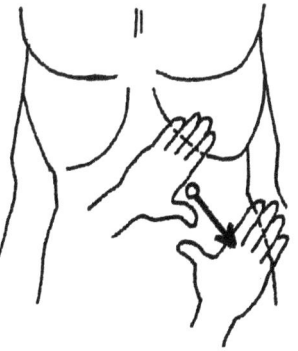

ULCERATED STOMACH

The patient should swallow the white of an egg thirty minutes before breakfast each morning for seven days. The stomach acids are so strong that they literally "cook" the egg white, coating the ulcer and allowing the patient to eat with a fair degree of comfort.

The treatment is given once a week for several weeks, until completely healed.

BED WETTING
and BLADDER WEAKNESS

Certain nerve centers that are out of their normal position cause a weakness that fails to give a warning urge that the bladder is ready to expel.

The nerves are located in cavities underneath the lower edge of the pubic bone, one on each side. When the index finger has contacted the cavity, press quite firmly upward, toward the head.

This treatment is used for dribbling of urine in adults and for bed wetting in children over the age of five years. Children younger than five years of age should NOT be treated.

BURNING SENSATION WHILE URINATING

A sagged condition of the abdominal tissue, making a visible crease one or two inches above the pubic bone, may be suspected. This condition can kink the urethra, not allowing the bladder to empty completely. The retained urine concentrates and becomes odorous.

While urinating, a person may use the fingers to stroke gently upward, along the center line of the body from the pubic bone to below the navel. The intent is to lift the tissues and straighten the urethra, allowing the bladder to empty completely. When lifting tissues the gentlest stroke is the most effective.

FEMALE DISORDERS

Inflamed Abdomen
Before beginning any treatment, check the abdomen to be sure the temperature is normal to your touch. Never massage an abdomen that is a warmer temperature than the rest of the body.

Instead, use the hand to draw the heat out by passing the open palm covered with olive oil about one inch above the abdomen, continuously, until the body temperature is reduced. Stop further treatment until another time.

Mr. Stephenson's Insights
There are three secretions of the vagina which control the purity of that organ. One of the three is a very strong cleansing fluid. The other two intermingle with it to heal any injuries and the third keeps that part of the body lubricated.

When one of the milder gland oils fails to perform its function, a burning sensation is felt in the vagina. If both fail to function, then the more powerful one—the strong, cleansing secretion—will cause very severe burning and itching.

If the three secretions are functioning in balance, they will keep the area clean and healthy. Unnatural substances should never be used for cleansing or irrigation.

The FEMALE DRAINAGE MASSAGE TREATMENT is given for all female problems listed and would be good as a preventative measure for all women.

Female Treatment— Drainage Massage

Massage from the pubic bone diagonally upward and toward the sides of the body, over the ovaries. The hand moves slowly and as resistance and sensitivity is decreased, the fingers will penetrate more deeply into the tissue and a drainage of the tubes and ovaries will have been achieved. The patient's sensitivity is always the guide in this treatment.

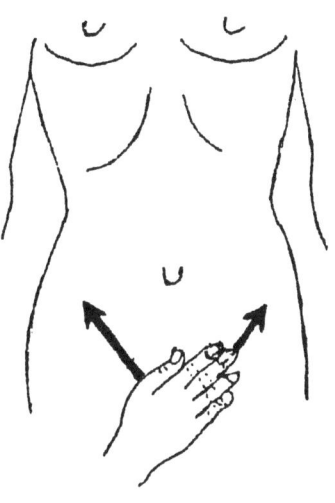

It is sometimes necessary to massage upward over the uterus by placing your open hand just above the pubic bone, being sure the palm is in contact as the hand moves very gently upward.

Next, give the treatment for bed wetting or bladder weakness in the dents on each side of the pubic bone.

There is also a nerve at the center of the lower edge of the pubic bone, similar to the one at the center of the chin. It can cause many problems if it has slipped out of its groove. It is easily replaced with the edge of the finger. This is something women can easily learn to check for themselves.

FEMALE DISORDERS

In addition to the Female Drainage Massage for regulating the three secretions many female problems are corrected with the drainage massage, bed wetting treatment and centering of the nerve, with a different emphasis depending on the problem.

Painful Menstruation
The most common problem pertaining to the reproductive system of the female body is that of painful menstruation. In almost all cases this is simple to correct with a vacuum massage over the tubes and ovaries on each side of the abdomen. The FEMALE DRAINAGE MASSAGE TREATMENT should be given 2 or 3 days before the flow is expected to begin.

Regulating the Menstrual Cycle
This is done by regulating the number of days between the Female Drainage Massage treatment in relation to the start of the patient's menstrual cycle and the normal 28 day cycle.

The first treatment is given the day before the patient expects her period. The next treatment is given 25 days from the day the flow actually begins. It will be necessary to give the treatment in this order for three months.

Burning or Itching in and Around the Vagina or 'Dry Vagina'
Problems of this nature will often cause heat, not only in the abdomen but often both heat and redness at the mouth of the vagina and on the outside of the body. The cooling treatment described earlier must be given for the abdomen. The same cooling strokes

FEMALE DISORDERS

one inch above the vaginal opening will reduce the heat and redness quickly.

Follow the cooling treatment with the FEMALE DRAINAGE MASSAGE.

With the basic treatments for the reproductive system you have the tools and understanding of how to cope with many other problems related to the female body.

Tipped Uterus
Fallen or Exposed Bladder

The treatment for these problems is similar to the Fallen Stomach Treatment. It is even possible that these discomforts could be caused by a fallen stomach which would pressure the lower organs. However, lifting something too heavy is a more likely cause of the fallen bladder. Even losing weight too fast lets organs drop.

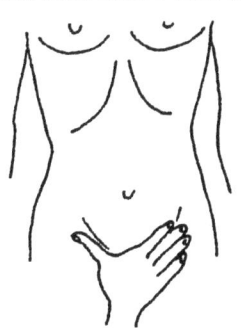

The treatment is similar in either case. To raise either uterus or bladder, place the well-oiled, open hand on it's edge, just above the pelvic bone and begin a very slow but firm movement upward. This creates a vacuum at the back of the hand which will draw the organs upward to their normal position.

For bearing down pain in the bladder or vagina, treat also the three spots at the pubic bone—the bed-wetting spots and the centering nerve.

FALLEN STOMACH

A fallen stomach is a condition of the digestive system that could cause great distress. The patient's build will help determine the possibility of this condition. The person will be thin and probably be long-ribbed, making the abdominal cavity much smaller.

Improper lifting most often causes the stomach to fall but the shock of an auto accident or a high fall can produce a fallen stomach. Also, losing too much weight too fast could cause the stomach to fall as the fat that cushions the vital organs is lost first, creating a space.

There is always a pulse beat felt on the abdomen when there is a fallen stomach. The location of the pulse will indicate how far the stomach has fallen.

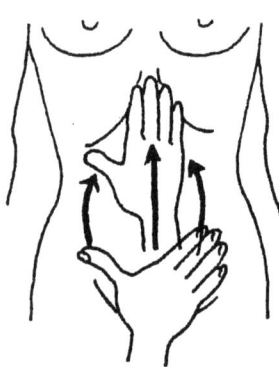

An "upward only" preparatory massage is given first. See ABDOMINAL MASSAGE. Remember: **TO MASSAGE DOWNWARD WOULD BE DANGEROUS!** The abdominal massage is applied for about ten minutes to equalize pressure and make the abdomen soft and pliable.

If the pulse beat has disappeared after the massage, it was tension that interfered with circulation and not a fallen stomach.

FALLEN STOMACH

If the pulse beat is still there continue with the stomach lift. Place the open hand, edges of the thumb and index finger just above the pubic bone. With a slow but firm movement upward, the whole hand eventually comes in full contact with the abdomen as it clears the pubic bone.

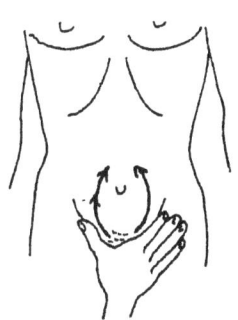

Depending on where the leading edge of the hand contacts the fallen stomach, the thumb and fingers, brought together in a kind of scissors movement, can coax the stomach to move upward. Continue the lifts three or four times until the stomach is in place and pulsation has stopped.

Apply a few minutes of massage as illustrated here to feed and strengthen the tissues that hold up the stomach and equalize the pressures in the abdomen.

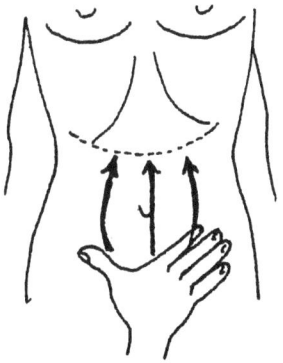

Follow up treatments should be given once a week for seven weeks.

REPRODUCTIVE ORGANS—
MALE AND FEMALE

There is a nerve center which controls the feed of nerve life to the reproductive organs, both male and female. This place must be checked and nerves centered, if necessary, in treatments for any female disorder or loss of manhood.

The nerve center to the reproductive organs is located one vertebra below the nerve that feeds the kidneys. Refer to KIDNEYS TREATMENT to locate the 'kidney spot'.

The treatment is a quarter twist with the thumb at the reproduction organ nerve center. so as to replace the nerve. Refer to the PAIN BETWEEN THE SHOULDERS for the quarter twist details.

As a man grows older, all the fluids are not expelled during an ejaculation. The secretion that remains behind coats the walls of the ejaculatory duct. The coating spreads and involves more and more of the surrounding ducts and tissues. Eventually, the congestion is carried to the prostate gland. It may become swollen, inflamed or abscessed.

For treatment, the man lies on his back, his legs partially flexed and spread. Using the middle finger and commencing forward of the anus, move the finger in a back and forth, zigzag motion across the median line, through the area of the scrotum, up to the base of the penis.

The contact is gentle but thorough. Slow the advance when thickened tissue or a sensitive area is encountered. After this zigzag motion, stroke 4 or 5 times along the full length of the same path. Repeat this cycle (1 zigzag to 5 strokes) for 4 times.

One application will frequently result in the passing of white "slime" or "eggshell" upon urination. This process needs only a good start by the treatment. Nature will complete it.

This treatment may be applied by the man himself. Several applications may be needed if the condition is severe. If a man uses this information and checks himself periodically, he will not need to worry about prostate trouble as long as he lives.

CRIPPLED LEGS

There are at least three causes for crippled legs that a Creative Healer may help relieve.

(1) If a person has lost partial or total use of a leg, it is a "crippled leg". If the loss is not from polio and there is any movement of the nerves in the groin area when the patient "thinks" movement, then this treatment will help.

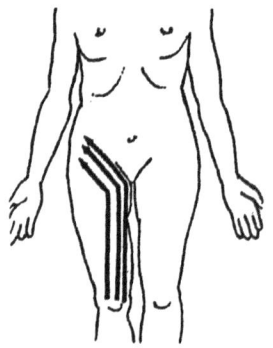

The problem will be found in the groin as you perform an upward massage from the knee, following the path of the sciatic nerve, fingers leading. Near the groin your fingers will encounter a hard lump. As you continue to massage (as illustrated) up and over the groin, the lump will get smaller. Finally it will move upward and slip into its normal position.

It is possible that both cartilage and nerve center have been forced out of position which indicates that the main artery to the leg had been constricted, If the muscles of the leg are not fed, they lose strength and cannot support the body.

After correcting the condition in the groin, massage the muscles of the leg from the knee to the groin in an upward direction for ten minutes. Massage from the ankle to the knee for another ten minutes using a strengthening massage, thumb separated from fingers to span the leg.

CRIPPLED LEGS

If the patient has control of the leg with his knee flexed as he lies on the bed, he will be able to walk. If the leg falls outward when flexed, more strengthening massage is needed.

If the patient can move both legs but cannot walk, both the groin and the spine must be treated.

(2) A crippled leg may also be caused by a soft vertebra just above the upper sciatic nerve on the spine.

Never use pressure directly on the vertebra. A gentle, feeding massage with the thumbs, moving toward the spine, will feed the vertebra and make it strong. Do not be discouraged if several treatments are needed to restore the legs to usefulness.

(3) Another possible cause of crippled leg may be the sciatic nerve as it comes out of the bone under the hip. A pressure or a pinch on this nerve center could cause it to become inflamed and thus cut off the life line to the leg.

The patient lies on his stomach. The Creative Healer first relieves the muscular contractions under the buttocks. (Described in the treatment for LOWER SCIATICA)

When these muscles are relaxed, you must draw the nerve into place. Place the finger of your right hand in the crease just under the buttocks on the patient's left side. With the pressure of your finger toward the left, the nerve will slip into position. Use the thumb on the right side, with pressure towards the patient's right side.

CARTILAGE OF THE KNEE

The patient sits facing the Creative Healer. His leg is carefully positioned with the knee slightly flexed as in the sketch.

A gentle massage is given using both hands. Draw the hands, thumbs together, over the area of the knee, then fingertips together, draw the hands down the underside of the knee. This will draw out heat and inflammation.

When the swelling has been reduced, use the flat of the fingers in a circular, breaking up movement, behind the knee in the popliteal space. Stroke downward to move the decongested material into the calf circulation.

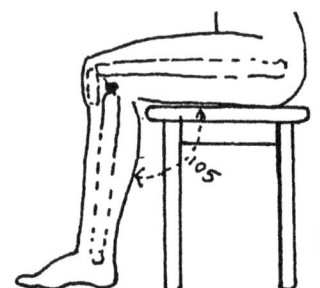

Place the forefingers in two little cavities, one on each side of the knee at the joint. With your elbows on your knees for stability, press in until the cartilages yield and move into place.

Strengthen the whole area with more downward massage.

VARICOSE VEINS

If varicose veins are present behind the knee, do not massage or press on them. Direct the breaking up movements along the side of such veins. The effect will penetrate to the region beneath the vein.

ANKLE FILTER TREATMENT

One of the main filters in the circulatory system is located at the ankle. The blood must flow from the larger blood vessels of the leg to the smaller ones of the foot and toes, so the importance of this filter cannot be overlooked. It is necessary to clean out the filter to treat poor circulation successfully.

The sketch shows the exact location of the gland that functions as a filter. Place the forefinger in the cavity at the ankle and massage with circular movement and a slight downward pressure to get the blood flowing throught the filter and to the feet.

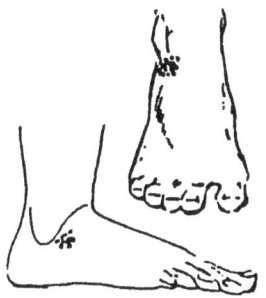

If varicose veins are very bad, treat only one minute at first or too much bad blood will be forced into the foot. The gentle, sprained-ankle massage, starting lower on the leg, is given with the filter cleaning treatment.

Patients may do this for themselves periodically. It will help warm up cold feet.

SPRAINED ANKLE

A sprained ankle means that the cartilage at the ankle joint is out of position.

The patient's foot is supported on the Creative Healer's towel-covered arm as in the sketch. Massage gently with plenty of olive oil from midway on the leg through the toes, drawing out all the heat and inflammation. While reducing the swelling the ankle filter will be cleaned as a finger passes through it.

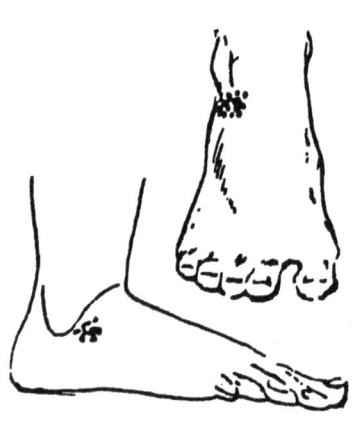

After the heat and swelling has been reduced, place the finger directly in the filter cavity while holding the foot firmly with the other fingers. Maintain this hold and with the other hand rotate the foot inward, down and around in one continuous motion.

This rotation of the foot opens the joint as the finger presses the cartilage into place.

BUNIONS

This is a condition where cartilage has protruded out of the joint at the base of the big toe. It is usually due to ill-fitting shoes. If not corrected, the joint oil seeps out into the flesh. This is a poison to the flesh and inflammation and pain will result.

The problem can be corrected if it is not of too long standing.

Hold the toe in such a way that the joint involved is as open as possible. Then with the thumb placed on the bunion, begin to press, gently at first, but slowly increasing the pressure until the cartilage goes back into place inside the joint. Rotate the toe, and massage to bring the circulation into the area.

If the repositioning is to last, the person must wear proper shoes. The shape of the shoe on the side of the big toe needs to be long enough to accommodate the big toe without bending it.

Nylon hose must also be long enough and have plenty of stretch. If shoes and hose are too short or shoes have pointed toes, bunions will be the result.

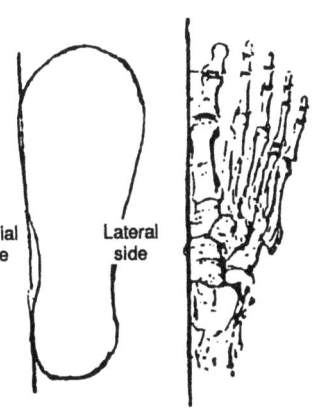

Right foot

ABOUT MR. STEPHENSON

If you have studied this introductory course in Creative Healing or have read this book with interest, you will want to know something about the man who had such knowledge of the human body that he could teach others his unorthodox methods of healing and of "seeing" the way the body functions.

Joseph Bestford Stephenson was born in Wylam on the river Tyne, near New Castle, England. He had very little formal schooling, because at an early age, he went to work in the coal mines. After coming to the United States at age 36, he worked in the coal mines of Pennsylvania and was quickly promoted to a position of responsibility.

He knew from a very early age that his life would sometime be devoted entirely to healing. Until age 49 his gift of healing was used after working hours for friends and neighbors. His life work of healing began in Johnstown, Pennsylvania, in 1923 when he rented a large, three story house for his work and his family.

Mr. Stephenson's day began very early, according to his son, and ended around ten at night. "Mealtimes were the only family time I remember" he said. "At ten my father would go into his study where he spent most of the night in silence or writing. He probably slept no more than two hours each night."

Because he was so busy with the many people coming to him for help, he did not ask his patients about symptoms. He knew the minute he saw them what needed to be done. In spite of the fact that he had no teacher, book nor formal training, his work as a

ABOUT MR. STEPHENSON

healer came very naturally to him as though he had always known how to do it. According to the records kept by his wife he treated as many as 60 persons a day, until at age 70 he retired to Long Beach, California, to devote his remaining years to teaching.

The healing work came so naturally to him that when he began to teach he first had to determine what it was in each treatment that made it so successful and then how to bring it to the student's level. The charts on the inside covers of this book are really masterpieces—because in those charts are the secrets of restoring health by touching.

Mr. Stephenson's work encompassed much more than the work of this booklet. In addition to the hands-on level of healing (which he considered the first level of healing) he had the ability to treat when the patient's condition was such that he could not touch (his second level of healing). In addition, time and place meant nothing to him and if the patient could not come to him—he could go to the patient instantly, (the third or 'absent' level of healing). Many of these cases occurred after he moved to California when former patients would telephone him from Pennsylvania.

Mabel Young, to whom this book is dedicated, said, "I have a very vivid memory of him in his later years when he mentioned to me that he had contracted a fatal disease. What could he possibly mean?"

"Well," he said, "This fatal disease is OLD AGE and there is no remedy for it." "It is 'Old Man Time' taking his toll. It is alright with me. I will not try to live nor will I try to die, but wait patiently until my heart stops, knowing it is the soil calling back to the soil. When the Soul-Mind is released from this old body, it will begin a new journey and live again."

In 1956, after a brief two day period in an unconscious state, Mr. Stephenson's Soul-Mind was released. His body was buried at Forest Lawn Memorial Park in Los Angeles, California.

Joseph Bestford Stephenson was a Man of Wisdom. We have had men of wisdom up through the ages, but they have been few. Mr. Stephenson wrote, "The Path of Wisdom is so hard, so steep, so rugged, so seemingly impossible to man that few have found it. It is a path you must travel alone. It is a path that two cannot travel together as no two men see alike. Other men can tell you of it, start you upon it, but that is as far as they may go."

The Joseph B. Stephenson Foundation was established to preserve, document and disseminate Mr. Stephenson's work in Creative Healing as well as his published and unpublished writings on other subjects.

To contact The Joseph B. Stephenson Foundation:
creativehealing@hotmail.com

To learn more:
www.stephensonscreativehealing.org

INDEX

A
Abdomen, inflamed, 86
Abdominal massage, 76
Abdominal massage, caution, 76
Acid stomach, heartburn, 79
Acute indigestion, 48
Adenoids, 19
Ankle filter treatment, 97
Antrum spots, location, 20
Asthma, 63

B
Back, lower (illus.), 67
Bearing down pain, 75
Bed wetting, 85
Binder, for asthma, 64
Binder, for babies, 64
Binder, for new mothers, 64
Binder, for weight loss, 64
Bladder problems, causes, 89
Bladder weakness, 85
Bladder, dribbling, 85
Bladder, fallen, exposed, 89
Bloodshot eyes, 27
Body maintenance, 82
Bowel consciousness, 74
Breathing trouble, babies, 64
Breathing tube, 59
Breathing tube, acid stomach, 60
Breathing, diaphragmatic, 60
Bunions, 99

C
Cartilage replacement, ankle, 98
Cartilage replacement, elbow, 44, 45
Cartilage replacement, groin, 94
Cartilage replacement, knee, 96
Cartilage replacement, shoulder, 43
Cartilage replacement, wrist, 46
Catarrh, 17
Chronic low back pain, 66
Cod liver oil, 62
Constipation spots, 67, 72
Constipation, 72
Constipation, babies, 72
Constipation, tight clothing, 61
Cough, tiring, unproductive, 63
Crippled legs, 94

D
Digestion, poor, 61

Digestive functioning, 82
Digestive tune-up, 82
Double vision, 26
Douches, 86
Dry cough, 25
Dry vagina, 88

E
Ears, wax build up, 20
Eno fruit salts, 80
Epilepsy, 39
Eyes, feeding, 26
Eyes, protruding, 27, 56, 58
Eyes, red or congested, 27
Eyes, tired or strained, 28
Eyes, withdrawing from, 27

F
Face lift, 29
Face pain, 30
Face pain, causes, 31
Facial tissues, 29
Failing eyesight, 26
Fallen stomach, 90
Feeding arms, 41
Female disorder, prevention, 86
Female disorders, 86
Female secretions, 86
Filter area, ankle, 98
Filter area, neck, 16
Filter area, wrist, 46
Filter areas, 16, 46, 98
Filters, function, 97
Finger exercise, caution, 47
Fingers, replacing cartilage, 47
Fingers, swollen joints, 46
Fingers, white, skin taut, 47
Flattened nostrils, 19
Flu spot, 37

G
Gall bladder, 78
Gall, liver connection, 78
General treatment, 15

H
Hay fever, 18
Headache, 38
Hearing loss, 20
Heart murmur causes, 54
Heart murmur, 54

Heart spot on back, 56
Heart tube, 51
Heart, 48
Heart, and gas, 48
Heart, basic treatment, 48
Heart, distribution centers, 50
Heart, fast, 53, 56
Heart, leaking, 52
Heart, pump-like, 52
Heart, regulating speed of, 53
Heart, slow, 54
Hemorrhoids, 73
Hemorrhoids, causes, 73
Hemorrhoids, itching cause, 74
Hiccough, 60
High and short breathing, 59
High blood pressure, cause, 33

I
Inward goiter, 56

K
Kidneys, 65

L
Laryngitis, 24
Legs, feeding muscles, 94
Liver, 77
Lung congestion, 62

M
Massage, caution, 90
Menstrual cycle, 88
Menstrual pain, 88
Migraine, 40
Migraine, pain description, 40
Milk, 62

N
Neck, importance of, 33

O
Olive oil, use of, 14

P
Pain, arms, 41
Pain, between shoulders, 36
Pain, elbow, 44
Pain, vaginal, 89
Pancreas, 79
Pancreas, feeding, 80

Pneumonia, 62
Prostate gland, 93
Pulse beat in abdomen, 90

Q
Quarter twist, 36
Quinsey, 23

R
Reproductive organs, 92

S
Sciatic nerve, lower, 68
Sciatic notches, 67
Sciatic nerve, upper, 70
Sciatica, 68
Shoes and hose, 99
Sinus, 17
Sinus, caution, 18
Soft vertebra, 95
Soft vertebra, caution, 95
Solar plexus, nerve center, 59
Spleen, 81
Sprained ankle, 98
Strep throat, 23
Sweating, excessive, 32

T
Thyroid importance, 55
Thyroid treatment, 56
Thyroid, Stephenson's concept, 56
Tight clothing marks, 61
Tonsils, 22

U
Ulcerated stomach, 83
Ulcers, use of egg whites, 84
Urination, burning, 85
Uterus, fallen, tipped, 89

V
Vaginal burning, itching, 88
Varicose veins, 96
Vitamin D, 62
Voice loss, 24, 25

W
Wrist, 46

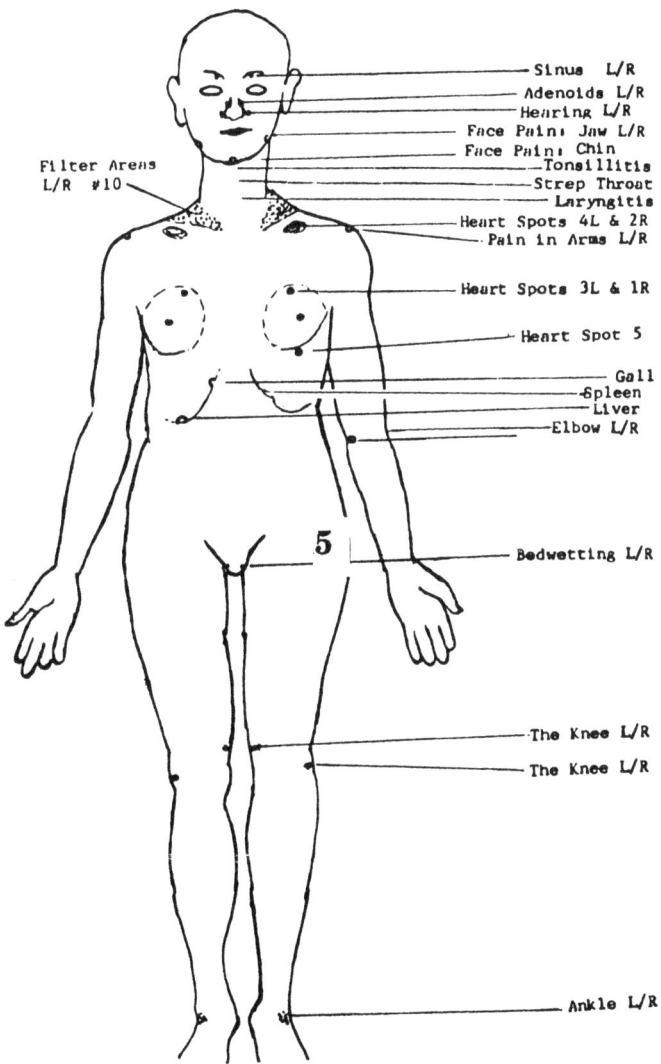

PRINCIPAL LOCATIONS
for Creative Healing applications on the
FRONT OF THE BODY

L/R indicates symmetrical locations on both left and right.

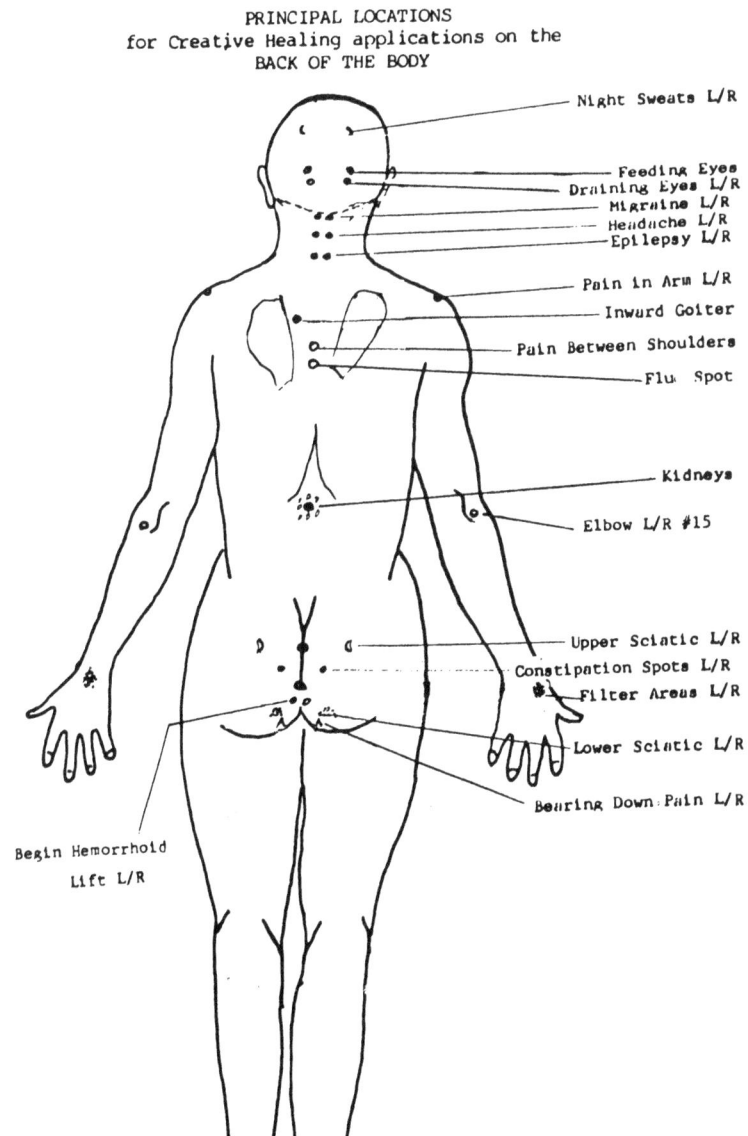

NOTES

NOTES

www.ingramcontent.com/pod-product-compliance
Ingram Content Group UK Ltd.
Pitfield, Milton Keynes, MK11 3LW, UK
UKHW022215230426
12048UKWH00016BA/861